THE CATHRIS GROUP

Solution Validation & Testing

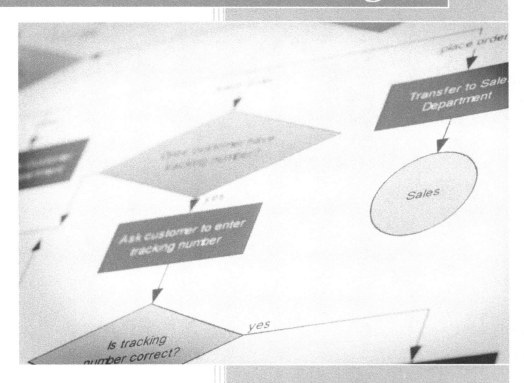

Martin Schedlbauer, Ph.D., CBAP, OCUP

www.cathris.com

Solution Validation & Testing
Published by
The Cathris Group
Sudbury, Massachusetts
www.cathris.com

Library of Congress Cataloging-in-Publication Data

ISBN-13: 978-1468134858
ISBN-10: 146813485X

Schedlbauer, Martin J.
   Solution Validation & Testing
M. Schedlbauer
   p.cm
Includes index.

1. Software Testing 2. Quality Assurance

Table of Contents

Testing Essentials

Upon completion of this chapter you will be able to:

✓   Describe the difference between testing, quality control, and quality assurance
✓   Define the role and skills of an effective tester
✓   Write testable requirements
✓   Decide whether to obtain a certification

Motivation

Validating a solution is essential to assuring the quality of the final deliverable. While solutions, particularly software solutions, are unlikely to ever be constructed without flaws, we nevertheless must strive to make them as robust as possible. Minor flaws might be tolerable as mere annoyances, but others can significantly compromise the value of the solution. Some flaws might even expose users to harm. Just consider flaws in healthcare systems, drug delivery devices or banking applications.

It is the responsibility of the Business Analyst, Testers, and End Users to ensure that the developed or acquired solution meets the needs of the business and that it solves the business problem or achieves the business objectives. This course demonstrates techniques to assure that the solution meet specific levels of quality. The quality of a solution is the degree to which it adheres to the stated requirements. No solution will meet 100% of its stated requirements, which means that stakeholders must agree on an acceptable level of quality.

Quality Control Versus Quality Assurance

Increasing the quality of a solution is done through two separate but equally important approaches:

- **Quality Control**. Quality Control is the process of determining whether the software works as required. It identifies scenarios where the outputs of the solution are below an acceptable level of quality. The primary means of quality control is testing. A significant part of test planning is the definition of acceptable output. Once a defect has been detected, the Business Analyst must work with the testing team to determine the root cause of the defect, assess the severity of the impact, and the probability of occurrence of the defect. Some defects may need to be resolved while others may be mitigated through work-arounds, manual activities, or may simply be acceptable.

- **Quality Assurance**. Quality Assurance is a set of practices that removes defects prior to testing. Code reviews, design reviews, requirements reviews, inspections, audits, pair programming, and formal proofs of correctness are common techniques to assure that quality is "built-in".

This course addresses both strategies, but places emphasis on quality control through testing, particularly user acceptance testing, for solution validation.

Quality control and quality assurance apply to any solution but this course focuses primarily on software solutions. These software solutions may be newly developed, acquired from a third party, or may be modifications to an existing solution.

Note that the terms quality control and quality assurance are often confused. In fact, many organizations call their testing groups quality assurance (or QA) groups, or simply QA. This isn't really the case as most of these groups are testing, a form of quality control, rather than performing static reviews or other quality assurance activities.

Terminology

There are several common terms used to describe solution defects. They all indicate that the solution, most commonly a software application, does not meet its requirements.

- bugs
- faults
- problems
- issues
- error
- failure
- incident
- anomaly
- variance
- inconsistency
- feature
- egg

The terms solution, software solution, software, software application, or simply application are used interchangeably in this course.

Definition: Defect

A solution defect is defined in the BABOK®[1] as follows:

> "A defect is a deficiency in a product or service that reduces its quality or varies from a desired attribute, state, or functionality. "

This type of defect is detected through testing. However, often a solution meets the requirements but is still unacceptable to the end user or other stakeholders. This happens when some of the requirements were stated incorrectly, not fully understood, or may have changed over time. The BABOK® defines a requirements defect as follows:

> "A requirements defect is an error in requirements caused by incorrect, incomplete, missing, or conflicting requirements."

Such defects are detected through quality assurance practices such as verifying requirements through reviews or simulations.

In practice, a defect is present when any one of these statements is true:

---

[1] In this course, the term BABOK® refers to the *Business Analysis Body of Knowledge Version 2.0* published by the International Institute of Business Analysis.

1. The solution does not perform as required by its specification.
2. The solution contains features that are not part of the specification.
3. The solution does not meet unstated but assumed requirements.
4. The solution's functionality is not accessible to its end users because it is too difficult to use, too slow, or otherwise not usable.

Sources of Defects

There are several causes of defects in solutions: incomplete, inconsistent, conflicting, or poorly stated requirements specifications, bad solution design, or mistakes in coding. Several studies have pointed out that the majority of bugs are traceable back to bad requirements.

Role of the Tester

The role of the tester is pretty simple: find as many defects as possible in the time allotted for testing and report the defects to the development team. The role of the tester is not solely to confirm that the software works. In fact, just because no defects have been uncovered during testing does not imply that the solution does not have any defects.

A tester is a role on a project team and not necessarily a job title. Some testers are dedicated quality assurance specialists while most others conduct testing as part their job. For example, many business analysts moonlight as testers, particularly on projects where there is not enough work for a dedicated testing resource.

Traits of Good Testers

While there are many traits that make a good tester, many effective testers:

- Are excited to explore software applications
- Are methodical and detail-oriented
- Test not just for what should work, but also look for unusual usage patterns
- Try to break things
- Work diligently in the time allotted for testing
- Know how to communicate defects so that they can be traced to their source and repaired
- Are creative and not afraid to test unusual scenarios

Writing Testable Requirements

Effective testing presumes effective requirements. The tester cannot validate what has not been defined. Therefore, effective testing starts with writing good requirements that are clear, unambiguous, and specific. At the end of the day, a requirement is nothing more than a precise statement of the expected behavior of the solution.

Requirements Definition

A requirement is simply a feature that a product or service must have in order to be useful. For example, two requirements for a customer relationship management system might be to allow users to update the payment terms for an account and to add new customers.

The IEEE Glossary of Software Engineering Terminology provides a more precise definition. The same definition is also used by the BABOK®. Both define a requirement as a

1. *condition or capability needed by a user to solve a problem or achieve an objective.*
2. *condition or capability that must be met or possessed by a system or system component to satisfy a contract, standard, specification, or other formally imposed document.*
3. *documented representation of a condition or capability in (1) or (2).*

Not all requirements are expressed at the same level of detail and specificity. Some might be high level requirements expressed by the business sponsor (*e.g.*, reduce the cost of invoicing customers) while others might be very specific requirements that describe a function needed by a particular user (*e.g.*, allow me to click on a customer name and then display that customer's account history).

Requirements Classification

The BABOK® defines the following requirements types: business, stakeholder (or user), functional solution, non-functional (or quality of service), solution, constraint, and transition[2].

Note that these terms are overloaded and have different meaning in different organizations. For example, a stakeholder requirement is often referred to as a business requirement in some organizations and a business requirement is sometimes called a business goal or project objective. Functional solution requirements are also often called technical requirements, detailed requirements, or system requirements. So, it is important to understand the semantics of the terms being used.

Business Requirement

A business requirement is a higher-level requirement that defines a business objective or goal for the project or initiative. For example, a business requirement for installing an asset-tracking system at a University might be to "reduce theft or misplacement of fixed assets by 10% each year."

---

[2] See Section 1.3.3.1 of the BABOK® Version 2.0

Business requirements describe the reasons for initiating a project. Each stakeholder requirement must be traceable back to a business requirement in order to be considered in-scope.

Stakeholder Requirement

A stakeholder requirement defines the need of a particular stakeholder, such as a project sponsor, end user, or regulatory body. These requirements are commonly defined through use cases as they describe how a stakeholder intends to interact with the solution. Stakeholder requirements define product features. For example, a stakeholder requirement for an asset-tracking system at a University might be to "allow IT Specialists to record fixed assets."

Solution Requirement

Solution requirements describe specific characteristics of the solution both in terms of functionality and quality of service. Solution requirements are sub-classified into functional and non-functional requirements.

Functional Requirement

Functional solution requirements define details of the expected behavior of the solution. For example, a functional solution requirement for an asset-tracking system at a University might be to "display each asset's ID, description, acquisition cost, current location, previous locations, and current responsible party."

Non-Functional Requirement

A non-functional solution requirement defines a quality of service requirement such as those relating to speed, response time, throughput, usability, security, privacy, availability, and so forth. For example, a non-functional solution requirement for an asset-tracking system at a University might be to "display an asset's current location and responsible party within 2 seconds after having its QR code scanned 90% of the time."

Transition Requirement

Transition requirements express how the solution will be placed into service and how to transition from the current state of the organization to its future state. These requirements, unlike the others, are temporary and require that the solution exist. For example, a transition requirement for an asset-tracking system at a University might be to "enter asset information from the current file records into the asset-tracking system through manual data entry."

SMART Requirements

Writing requirements that follow the *SMART* template is a good starting point. *SMART* requirements are specific, measurable, achievable, relevant, and testable. Note that there are alternate but equally valid definitions of *SMART* used in practice. SMART requirements apply equally to functional as well as non-functional (quality of service) requirements.

Specific

A good requirement is specific and does not rely on generic or vague terms and descriptions. It should be precise enough to avoid being misinterpreted and be non-compound. In other words, a requirements definition should state a single requirement, so conjunctions such as "and", "or", "except", and so forth should be avoided. Split the requirement into several requirements if necessary.

Measurable

The requirement must specify a metric that can be measured. Common metrics are time, performance, response time, volume, and so forth.

Achievable

The requirement must be attainable; in other words it cannot state a condition or capability that cannot be implemented.

Relevant

The requirement must address some need and must be traceable back to a business objective. It must be relevant to the project. This attribute helps manage project scope by only considering requirements that address an actual objective.

As a challenge question ask the stakeholders: "If this requirement were not implemented, would we still be able to achieve all of our business objectives?" If the answer is yes, then the requirement is not relevant and should be considered out-of-scope (or at least low priority).

Testable

A test can be devised that determines whether the requirement has been implemented.

Examples of SMART Requirements

The online course registration portal shall allow students who register for courses but have an outstanding balance to pay the balance online using one or more U.S. bank issued Visa, MasterCard, or American Express credit cards as long as the outstanding balance is less than $1,000.

The asset tracking system shall allow users authorized to view reports to generate an end-of-month report that includes a list of all currently deployed assets along with their last known location and responsible parties' full names.

Examples of Poor Requirements

Requirements that don't meet the *SMART* guidelines tend to be poor and lead to issues meeting the business and end users needs. Here are some examples of requirements that are not *SMART* compliant.

The system shall produce a periodic report that displays all asset data.

Why is this requirement poor? It does not specify what periodic means and it wants *all* data. *All* is too generic and creating a test for that would be difficult. What should happen if new fields were added to the assets' records? Would that invalidate that requirement? Can you devise a set of test scenarios that demonstrate that the asset tracking system meets these requirements fully?

The system shall provide immediate feedback when an asset's QR code has been scanned to indicate a successful scan.

This requirement is poor because the term immediate is impossible to implement. There is always a lag between the time and stimulus occurs (the barcode scan) and an action happens (the lookup of the asset and the display of its data).

Verification & Validation

These two terms are often used interchangeably, but they are not the same. They are often used in conjunction as software verification and validation (or V&V).

Verification is the process of making sure that the requirements are correct, while *validation* is the process of confirming that the solution meets the requirements. Simply put:

> *Verification ensures that we build the right solution, whereas validation confirms that we built the solution right.*

Relevant Standards

For more industry best practices and standards on how to write testable requirements, test plans, and set up test strategies, consult the standards in Table 1:

TABLE 1. TESTING STANDARDS

Standard	Description
IEEE Standard 610.12-1990	Glossary of Software Engineering Terminology
IEEE Standard 730-2002	Standard for Software Quality Assurance Plans
IEEE Standard 828-2005	Standard for Software Configuration Management
IEEE Standard 829-2008	Standard for Software and System Test Documentation
IEEE Standard 830-1998	Recommended Practices for Software Requirements Specifications
IEEE Standard 1008-1987	Standard for Software Unit Testing

IEEE Standard 1012-2004	Standard for Software Verification and Validation
IEEE Standard 1028-2008	Standard for Software Reviews and Audits
ISO9241-1:2002	Ergonomic Requirements for Office Work With Visual Display Terminals

BABOK® Cross Reference

This topics in this course generally align with Section 7 of the BABOK® Guide Version 2.0 and the *Solution Assessment and Validation* Knowledge Area.

Certifications

As demand for software testing and quality assurance professionals is increasing, so is the need for independent certification of skills. Unlike other disciplines, in the field of the testing there are numerous certifications. The most common certifications for practitioners are listed in Table 2. Additional certifications for managers are available through the same organizations.

TABLE 2. SOFTWARE TESTING CERTIFICATIONS FOR PRACTITIONERS

Certification	Certification Body	Requirements
CSTE – Certified Software Test Engineer	QAI Global Institute www.softwarecertifications.org	IT Degree + Experience; Exam
CSTP – Certified Software Test Professional	IIST www.iist.org	Course Work + Experience; Exam
ITQSB – Multiple Levels	ITQSB www.itqsb.org	Experience; Exam
CASQ – Certified Associate in Software Quality	QAI Global Institute www.softwarecertifications.org	IT Degree + Experience; Exam
CSQA – Certified Software Quality Analyst	QAI Global Institute www.softwarecertifications.org	IT Degree + Experience; Exam

In addition to the above industry certifications, a number of testing tool vendors offer their own certifications. One of the most common is HP's QTP (QuickTest Professional) certification.

This course does not specifically prepare for any of these certifications. It is not an "exam cram" course, but it does provide enough knowledge and background to adequately prepare the participant for the *CSTE* exam administered through the *Quality Assurance Institute (QAI)*. Visit www.softwarecertifications.org for more information on how to apply for the CSTE certification. (Software Certifications, 2006)

Resources

Web Sites

Web Site	Description
www.istqb.com	International Software Testing Qualifications Board
www.testingsnews.com	Whitepapers and resources for software testing
www.softwaretestingnow.com	Tips, tools, and techniques for software testing
www.sqaforums.com	Online community of software testing and quality assurance professionals
www.utest.com	Online community for software testing

Social Networking

Social Network	Description
Twitter: @TestingsNews	News and articles about Software Testing and Test Automation using HP QTP

Crowdsourcing

Crowdsource	Description
www.pay4bugs.com	Crowdsourcing portal where organizations can "outsource" testing and pay per bug
www.utest.com	Resources for testers and access to crowdsourcing and outsourcing

Books

For books about testing, quality control, and quality assurance, consult the Bibliography at the end of the book.

Summary

- Testing is a critical phase in solution development
- Testing is one way to increase quality, another is through various quality assurance strategies
- Defects are deficiencies in products that must be uncovered, recorded, and communicated by the tester
- There are different types of requirements, but all should be defined following the *SMART* guidelines
- There are numerous certifications available for professionals that can attest to their testing skills and competencies

Case Study: Building a Cloud-Based CRM

Upon completion of this chapter you will be able to:

✓ Understand the case study and how it is used
✓ Work with the case study in upcoming workshop activities

Motivation

This chapter introduces the case study that will be used as a basis for examples as well as the workshop exercises. It is a simple web-based client relationship management (CRM) application for the yacht charter company *BoatVentures*. The CRM will be used as a basis for exploring various quality control and assurance strategies.

Background

Chris Kelly got his captain's license when he was still working as a yard helper in Southern Florida back in the early 1990's. His love for boats and the ocean was always strong and he promised himself that when he got older he would allow others to share his enthusiasm and make sure that he would stay connected to the water. So, when the chance arose in 1999 to join the crew of a large yacht owned by a wealthy technology entrepreneur, he did not hesitate. Although he was only a deckhand at first, he quickly demonstrated his seamanship, deck skills, and superb trouble shooting abilities in pressure situations. He was promoted to First Mate within a year and then when the position of ship's Master opened up he jumped at the chance. He got his 100GT USCG Master's License and ran the *Solitude* and managed its crew of four with a steady hand.

In 2005, Chris moved to Cape Cod with his fiancé so that she could be closer to her family. He took work in several yards around Falmouth, but was not happy. In 2006, he had a chance to buy a 38' sail boat that was being foreclosed on. He bought the boat with some savings and a sizable mortgage and decided to put the boat to work through chartering. His business increased rapidly and soon he was able to book more charters than he had time for. He bought two more boats: a 20' Mako center console for inland fishing charters and a 46' Maxum power yacht for cruises to the nearby islands of Martha's Vineyard, Nantucket, Cuttyhunk, Block Island, and the shores of Long Island. His charter company, *BoatVentures*, took off.

The Franklin Planner that Chris was using to track his captains, crew, bookings, guests, leads, and marine contractors was quickly becoming too cumbersome to use – particularly now that he had hired two part-time charter agents and had established relationships with several regional charter brokers. He was getting an increasing number of charter inquiries each day and had trouble tracking them in his Planner. The e-mails that his agents were sending him were piling up and he found that he often missed sales leads causing lost sales opportunities. In addition, Chris had trouble managing his contingent workforce of captains, deckhands, mates, and marine contractors.

He knew that there had to be a better way to manage his business. He researched a number of different booking systems, but none fit the special needs of a yacht charter company. It looked like he needed a custom solution. After consulting with some tech entrepreneurs he met as charter guests Chris decided to build his own solution. Chris hired *Interactive Solutions*, a Boston based web application development firm to build a custom CRM solution for his business. He also figured that he was not the only one facing these problems and that other charter operators may have similar issues. So, he negotiated a contract with *Interactive* that would allow him to offer his solution as a product to other charter operators. It's Chris' way of offsetting some (if not all) of the expenses associated with creating a custom software application. He was hoping that he might perhaps turn into a successful software entrepreneur in addition to charter operator *extraordinaire*.

Making the solution more generic and turning it into an actual product turned out to be a lot more challenging than Chris expected. He not only had to think of the features and functions that he needed but also what other charter companies might require. As his charter business was booming, he was simply too busy and not experienced enough to precisely define the requirements for his CRM system that *Interactive* asked for. So, Chris hired Monica Immerhof, a contract Business Analyst recommended to him by Jennifer Chan at *Interactive*. Monica proved to be immensely helpful and very capable. She quickly elicited the requirements and documented a comprehensive list of requirements, needs, and objectives for the project – now code named *Splash*.

The *Splash* initiative had two somewhat distinct but related technology efforts.

1. **Online Booking Management**. Update the corporate web site to make it easier for guests to create and manage their charter bookings online and without help by the charter agents.
2. **Corporate CRM**. Create a new charter bookings client relationship management (CRM) application capable of tracking guests, their bookings, our own as well as partner yachts, crew, and marine contractors. In addition, the CRM should serve as a central point for managing sales and marketing efforts.

The development team at *Interactive* was able to create working prototypes of the website and the CRM containing the major functional requirements within two weeks and a first delivery of *Splash* is scheduled at the end of next month. *Interactive* has substantially completed coding of the first iteration and is now entering a comprehensive testing phase of the product created thus far. To get around the limited resources available for testing, *Interactive* has outsourced the testing effort to a third party. While *Interactive* generally does all of its testing in-house, they simply do not have the resources to complete the project on the aggressive timeline set by Chris Kelly. An outsourcing partner is necessary and Chris quickly concedes.

The following sections list the information that Monica Immerhof has found and which form the basis for all testing and quality assurance effort by you, the outsourcing partner engaged by *Interactive*.

Business Requirements

There are a number of strategic goals for the *Splash* initiative at *BoatVentures*:

- Increase the closing rate of sales calls by 20% within the first year after deployment by tracking sales leads more accurately and using them for targeted marketing and sales efforts.
- Increase online charter bookings by 30% within two years after deployment by providing a self-service option on our web site.
- Increase the rate of repeat bookings within 12 months by 25% within the two years after deployment by tracking charter bookings more closely and offering promotions after completion of the charter.
- Derive a minimum of $20,000 in additional annual revenue from licensing the *Corporate CRM* to other charter operators.

Going forward, we will concentrate only on the *Corporate CRM* portion of the *Splash* initiative.

Vision Statement

The Corporate CRM will allow internal agents and external charter brokers to book charters for guests that directly call *BoatVentures* or a charter broker. The CRM will manage the booking. In addition, the CRM will manage all other aspects of running the charter operations, including yacht and crew management, marine contractors, and sales leads. Upon completion, the Corporate CRM will be the central portal for all operational aspects of *BoatVentures* and will be the exclusive platform for managing its business.

Glossary of Terms & Acronyms

Term	Definition
ZI	Zoho Invoice. The cloud-based invoicing solution used by *BoatVentures*.
QoS	Quality of Service. A non-functional type of solution requirement that includes usability, availability, and performance requirements, among others.
CRM	Customer Relationship Management
Time Charter	A charter in which the vessel is leased to the charter party for a specific duration of time and the vessel is under the full control of

	its Master and crew and all risk is borne by the owner of the vessel.
Master	The person in charge of the vessel and its crew; generally the Captain
Demise Charter	A charter in which the vessel is leased "bare boat" to the charter party and the charter party assumes all risk of loss. The charter party must supply its own crew and controls the vessel's destination.
OUPV	Operator of Uninspected Passenger Vessels. A type of license issued by the Coast Guard whose holder can carry up to six passengers on a hired vessel.
Vessel	A power or sail boat.
Agent	See Charter Agent
Charter Agent	An employee of *BoatVenture's* responsible for booking charters
Broker	See Charter Broker
Agency	See Charter Broker
Charter Broker	An external party who books charters for clients that are serviced by charter companies. Brokers can be individuals or brokerage firms
LOA	Length Overall. The total length of a vessel including its anchor pulpit and swim platform

Stakeholder Requirements

This section states the stakeholder requirements for the *Corporate CRM* portion of *Splash*. The section first defines the different stakeholders and then describes their specific user requirements as use cases.

Stakeholders

A stakeholder is any person or entity that is impacted by the project or has influence over it. The following stakeholders have been identified for the *Corporate CRM*:

Stakeholder	Role	Needs
Chris Kelly	Project Sponsor, Agent, Crew, Manager	Manage sales, schedules, crew, yachts, and vendors

Agents	End Users	Manage sales, schedules, crew, yachts, and vendors
Brokers	End Users	Ability to manage charters
Crew	End Users	Check schedules and assignments
Manager	End User	Manage crew, yachts, vendors, and assignments

User Requirements

The following use cases have been identified for each stakeholder group representing end users.

Actors

Actor	Definition
Agent	An employee responsible for booking charters; also known as Charter Agent
Broker	An external party who books charters for clients that are serviced by charter companies. Brokers can be individuals or brokerage firms; also known as Charter Broker or Agency
Manager	An employee with additional authorities
Crew	Employees or contractors who are run yachts. Crew includes deckhands, operators, Captains, Chefs, stewards and stewardesses
Administrator	An employee or contractor responsible for managing the system and security roles and privileges

Use Case Catalog

Actor	Use Cases
Agent	• UC01: book a charter • UC02: update a booking • UC03: view available yachts • UC04: track lead • UC05: view booking schedule • UC06: manage to-do list

Broker	Acts in the role of *Agent*, plus: • UC11: view earned commissions
Manager	Acts in the role of *Agent* and *Crew*, plus: • UC21: assign crew • UC22: add yacht • UC23: update yacht profile • UC31: add maintenance item • UC32: update maintenance item • UC41: add marine contractor • UC42: update marine contractor
Crew	• UC61: view assignments • UC62: view crew profile • UC63: update crew profile
Administrator	• UC71: manage user accounts • UC72: manage authorizations

Use Case Diagrams

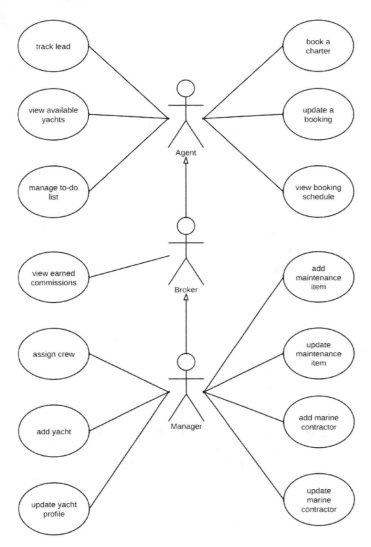

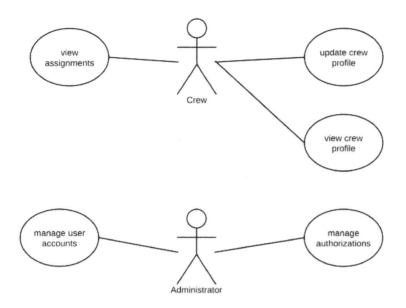

Use Case Narratives

This section contains narratives for selected use cases. Each narrative is comprised of a brief description of the use case, its scenarios, and scripts of the normal and major alternate and exception scenarios. In addition, pre and post conditions are listed. Where appropriate, an activity diagram of the flows is provided.

UC01: Book a Charter

Description:	A charter agent books a charter on behalf of a guest. The charter is for a yacht that meets the needs of the charter guest. For demise charters, the agent also books a crew for the guest if desired. Note that charter guests can also book charters online on their own, but this use case covers charters booked by agents.

Author:	MI	*Version:*	1.0	*Priority:*	4
Perspective:	O *Current State* ⊙ *Future State*			*Type:*	System
Duration:	Minutes	*Frequency*:	Daily	*Status*:	Implemented

Pre Conditions:
- Guest has a valid profile
- A yacht meeting the guest's needs is available
- Crew is available for the desired charter dates

Scenarios:
- Successful booking of yacht and crew
- No yacht is available for the desired charter dates
- No crew is available for the desired charter dates

*Example
Scenario:*
Charles Murphy is vacationing on Cape Cod and wants to take his family for a day trip to Nantucket. He does not have a computer available and decides to call *BoatVenture's* reservation number that he got from his hotel's concierge. Rick Tierney, one of *BoatVenture's* charter agents, picks up the phone and works with Charles to book the charter. He asks him for his preferred date, the number of guests in his party, and his destination. Once the charter details have been confirmed, Rick books the charter and reserves the yacht for Charles and his family.

Normal Path:
1. This use case starts when a request for a charter has been received (telephone, fax, or e-mail)
2. The agent logs into the system using a password {*V1*}
3. The system ask the agent for the charter dates
4. The system displays a list of available yachts for the selected dates
5. The system asks the agent for a list of yacht outfitting preferences
6. The system applies the filter and displays yachts matching the preferences
7. The agent selects a yacht
8. The system asks for the number of charter guests {*V2, V3*}
9. The system calculates the charter cost
10. The system asks for the charter parties' name, billing information, and e-mail address
11. The system ask for credit card information to charge a deposit
12. The system asks the agent to specify crew {*V4*}
13. The agent selects the crew required {*B008*}
14. The system adds the assignment to each crew member's schedule
15. The system sends a message to each crew member informing them of the new assignment
16. The system adds the reservation to the yacht's schedule
17. The system adds the charter to each crew member's schedule
18. This use case ends when a confirmation of the charter has been sent to the charter party

Variations:
V1: Credentials not Valid

1. The system displays an error message
2. The agent is not permitted to continue
3. Use case aborts

V2: More than 6 Charter Guests

1. The system displays an informational message that this requires booking a demise charter requiring separate crew
2. The agent presents a list of crew alternatives to the charter party
3. The agent selects crew based on the crew requirements of the selected yacht
4. The agent assigns crew to the charter

5. Use case continues

V3: More than 12 Charter Guests

1. The system displays an error message as that exceeds the maximum allowed by Coast Guard regulations
2. The agent must update the number of guests or abort the use case

V4: No Crew Available

1. The system displays an informational message informing the agent that no crew is available for those dates
2. The agent must change the charter dates or mark the charter as tentative assuming suitable crew can be hired in time {B010}

Post Conditions:	• The charter has been booked and added to the list of reservations
	• The yacht has been reserved and the yacht's booking schedule has been updated
	• The crew has been assigned and the crew's schedule has been updated
	• An e-mail message has been sent to all members of the assigned crew informing them of their new assignment
Related Requirements & Rules	R001, R002, R003, R004, R005, R006 B001, B003, B004, B007, B008, B010
Open Issues & Notes:	The credential scheme presently uses only a password to protect pages from unauthorized access; in the future *OAuth* or *OpenLogin* with Zoho integration should be used.

Prioritization Scheme

The use cases and associated requirements are prioritized based on a numeric score from 1 to 5, where 5 is the highest priority. A definition of the ranking scale is provided below.

TABLE 3. REQUIREMENTS & USE CASE PRIORITIZATION SCHEME

Score	Label	Definition
1	Not important	Lowest priority; the product functions well without it.
2	Nice to have	The product would be more usable and more competitive with the requirement included, but functions well without it
3	Useful	The requirement represents needed functionality, but that

		functionality can be deferred until a later release; there are workarounds available and the product is usable without it
4	Important	The requirement is very important, but workarounds exist. The product is compromised without it
5	Necessary	The requirement is critical and the product does not function without it; there are no workarounds

Solution Requirements

This section lists detailed solution requirements, including functional requirements not captured in the use case narratives. In addition, quality of service (non-functional) requirements are defined, including those relating to security, performance, usability, recoverability, and so forth.

Requirements Catalog

The detailed solution requirements are listed in the table below with a portion of the relevant and useful attributes. Additional attributes that will be added later include risk, responsible party, version, date created, level of difficulty, due date, linkage to business requirement, rationale for inclusion, and origin.

ID	Type	Definition	Stability	Priority
R001	QoS	The solution must support at least 10 concurrent transactions.	3	4
R002	Security	Access to the system is restricted to authorized parties and must be protected through passwords	3	5
R003	Functional	The solution must accept MasterCard, Visa, and American Express, but processing of credit cards is done through a separate merchant account platform	2	1
R004	Functional	Crew is informed of new crew assignment through an e-mail that is sent immediately upon booking the charter so that crew can work with the manager to change the schedule if necessary	3	3
R005	Functional	The solution should allow confirmation to be sent to charter parties via e-mail	4	2
R006	Functional	Confirmations of charters should include the date, time of departure, port of	3	3

	embarkation, time of return, Master/Captain's name and mobile number, address of port, selected destinations or itinerary, selected charter preferences, name of yacht, and list of items to bring to charter
R007	Functional

Stability is measured on a scale from 1 to 5, where 1 indicates a requirement that is likely to change in the short term, while 5 indicates a requirement that is unlikely to change in the long term.

The priority scheme is the same as for use cases and is defined Table 3.

Business Rules

Rule Catalog

ID	Definition	Exceptions	Source
B001	A time charter is restricted to a maximum of six passengers and none of the passengers must have paid a fare.	None	USCG
B002	A Master assigned to a vessel must have a USCG License of the appropriate tonnage and operating restrictions.	Crew that is hired by a private party to operate a private boat not carrying passengers for hire.	USCG
B003	A demise charter is restricted to a maximum of twelve passengers and must supply its own crew.	None	USCG
B004	All crew hired by a demise charter party must be approved by the vessel's owner.	Crew directly employed by *BoatVentures*	Kelly
B005	All Masters assigned to a vessel must have at least an OUPV license.	None	Kelly
B006	All vessels must have a gross tonnage less than 100GT.	Brokered yachts with crew in international waters	Kelly

B007	All charters require a 50% deposit upon booking and the remainder of the estimated charter amount is due prior to departure	None	Chris
B008	Vessels less than 30' LOA require only a Master. Vessels between 31' and 50' require a Master and at least one deckhand. Vessels above 50' require a Master and a deckhand for each deck.	If wait staff or chefs are requested, then these are added to the crew requirements for vessels above 50'	Chris
B009	Wait staff, stewards, stewardesses, and chefs may all act in the role of deckhand.	None	Chris
B010	A charter is marked as tentative if a deposit has not been received or crew has not been assigned to the charter.	Deposits may be waived if approved by a Manager	Chris

Constraints and Assumptions

- Billing of charters will be done through Zoho Invoice (ZI), a separate invoicing system that is already installed at *BoatVentures*. Eventually, the CRM will be integrated with ZI through Zoho's Application Programming Interface (API).
- Billing and payment processing is done through Square, a separately managed *iOS* application. It is expected that credit card processing will eventually be added directly to the CRM.

Risks

During elicitation the following risks have been identified as having the potential to significantly impact the initiative and either cause substantial delay or budget overruns. It is assumed that the risks catalog below will be expanded during development. The listed risks should be used to drive testing and quality assurance efforts.

ID	Definition	P	I	Strategy
K001	Integration of the *Zoho* database forms through the *Weebly* web hosting platform may not be fast enough to meet the performance requirements.	40%	80	Mitigate through a prototype Avoid by moving to *Caspio* or a PHP

based solution

P is the probability or likelihood of the risk occurring and is measured on a scale from 0% to 100%. *I* is impact which is measured on a scale of 1 to 9, where 9 is the most significant impact.

Accessing the Case Study

The prototype of the *Corporate CRM* delivered by *Interactive* can be accessed online at boatventures.weebly.com. It has been tested on a Mac with Chrome Version 15 but is expected to work on Safari and on Windows under the latest versions of Internet Explorer, Firefox, and Chrome.

To quickly access the *BoatVentures* prototype, scan the QR Code below in your tablet, mobile device, or desktop computer. On most scanning apps this will immediately launch a web browser and open the URL.

FIGURE 1. QR CODE FOR CASE STUDY WEB APPLICATION URL

Testing Strategies

Upon completion of this chapter you will be able to:

✓   Differentiate between different testing approaches
✓   Appreciate the role of testing in different project lifecycles
✓   Use incremental approaches to testing

Motivation

Most testers believe that it is their job to prove that a solution does not contain any defects. This is impossible; a program cannot be tested completely. There will always be some remaining defects.

Since testing everything is practically (and in many cases theoretically) impossible that implies that there remains a residual risk that defects linger in deployed solutions. Testing is therefore a risk reducing activity. While we might want to reduce the risk to zero, that may be cost prohibitive. We need to balance the cost with the amount of residual risk of defects we are willing to accept. The objective of a professional tester is to conduct the optimal amount of testing, balancing risk and cost.

Software defects tend to be clustered. Finding one defect in some area of a solution will likely reveal additional defects in the same module. Why is this the case? For one, programmers tend to make the same mistakes (these can often be found best through code reviews – a form of quality assurance discussed in a later chapter.) Another reason is that one defect can often cause other failures.

Once defects are found, they need to be documented and then removed. Often, removing defects may not be feasible: there's not enough time before release; it's not really a defect but rather an incorrectly stated requirement; fixing the defect may cause other parts of the solution to break and those failures are even worse; and finally, fixing the defect may just not be worth it – there are work-arounds that can be applied or the defect is simply not impactful enough. Defects that remain in the solution are referred to as *latent defects*.

Testing Approaches

Testing approaches can be broken down into two overall categories: static versus dynamic. Static tests perform analysis of the code while dynamic tests execute the code and observe its behavior to various stimuli. Static tests are a form of quality assurance and will be discussed in a later chapter. Dynamic tests rely on test cases and scenarios with various data inputs.

Dynamic tests can either rely purely on the externally observable behavior of the solution or be based on its internal implementation. Testing that is based purely on behavior are called *black-box tests* while those that inspect the internal structure of the solution are called *white-box tests*.

Tests can check the functionality or behavior of the solution or its qualities of service. Service (or functional/behavioral) tests determine if the solution performs according to its specification while quality of service (*QoS*) tests – also called non-functional tests – determine if the solution meets quality targets such as performance targets, security targets, usability targets, or scalability targets.

Testing presumes that there is a specification based on stakeholder requirements. The specification is used to create appropriate test cases and scenarios. In the absence of specifications or requirements documentation, testers may choose to conduct exploratory testing. Exploratory testing is an *ad hoc* testing approach that uses the intuition of the tester and principally looks for possible failures of the solution.

The different testing approaches are summarized in Figure 3.

Incremental Testing

Testing should be done incrementally from smallest to largest. This means that each component should be tested by itself to isolate component failures. Next, components are connected to other components in the same module and are tested together to assure that the module works. The modules are then tested as a complete system. Once the system has been demonstrated not to fail, the users perform final testing to ensure that the solution meets their needs. Finally, as changes are made to the solution, affected components and modules are re-tested to make sure that the system continues to function.

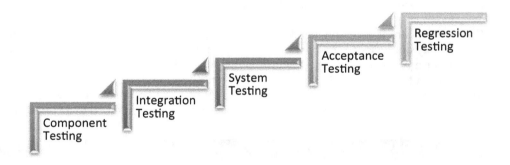

FIGURE 2. INCREMENTAL TESTING

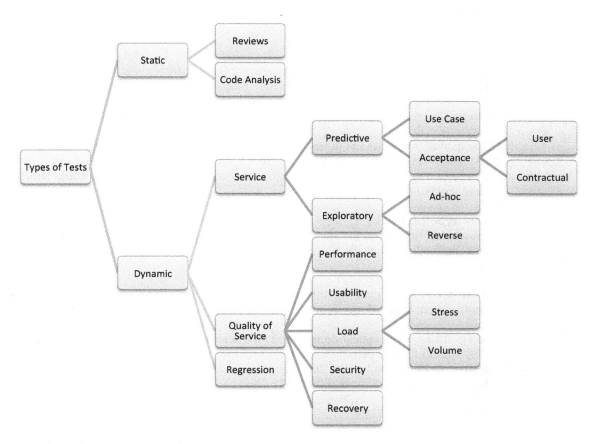

FIGURE 3. TAXONOMY OF TESTING APPROACHES

Component Testing

Component tests are performed in each unit of programming as it is developed, which is why these tests are also often called unit tests. These tests are generally done by the developer him or herself, although it is recommended that developers not test their own code whenever possible. Ideally, component test cases and test harnesses should be created before coding starts so that the specifications are fully formed and expressed.

Typical components tested by developers include functions, object methods, classes, or web services or other API (Application Programming Interface) calls. Testing of these components requires some kind of test harness, i.e., some programming scaffolding in which the code can be tested. Common test harness scaffolding used by Java developers is *JUnit*.

Component testing requires significant programming skills and is generally done by developers or software engineers. In mission critical system, a test engineer creates the test harness and performs the component testing.

Integration Testing

After component testing demonstrated that individual units function properly, the components are then connected to other components to form a module, use case, screen, or other higher-level structure. Programmers, software engineers, test engineers, or integration engineers typically do the work of connecting the components.

The goal of integration is to test that the components connect correctly and that faults in the interfaces are exposed. When a defect occurs it is generally in the interface between the components rather than the individual component implementations, which have been validated during component testing.

This type of testing is also valuable when testing web services or other remote communication protocols such as CGI interfaces built with PHP, JSP, ASP, Ruby on Rails, and so forth. In distributed systems, each layer should be tested individually and separately.

As with component testing, the testing team must create test harnesses that provide an environment in which the components can be connected and communicate.

Integration testing is best done in an incremental fashion; as components are developed they should first be tested individually and then as integrated units. Leaving integration testing until the end – the "big bang" approach – is not advisable because it makes finding defects much more difficult. The less code that is suspect the better.

System Testing

The next level of testing after integration testing is system testing. The previous testing was done from a specification perspective and geared towards correct implementation of the specification. System testing, on the other hand, is done from the users perspective. The tester validates that all of the requirements have been implemented correctly. In addition, testers look for conditions where the system does not behave as expected or might even fail or "crash". Misuse is also addressed during system testing.

System testing requires a full test environment complete with hardware, software, operating system, sample data, and all other infrastructure components that mimics the actual deployment environment. This test environment must be separate from the operational environment.

The test environment must not be connected to any live system components under any circumstances – a failed test should never disturb the operations of an organization.

System testing presumes a defined and approved set of requirements that define the expected behavior from the users or customers point of view. Proxies, for example, business analysts or project managers, often do this type of testing.

Acceptance Testing

Up to this point, the testing was under the control of the solution development team and was primarily carried out by members of that team. Acceptance testing is also often called user acceptance testing or UAT since it is generally performed by the actual users. The basis for testing is the requirements specification or some other contractual agreement.

Acceptance testing is typically the final step prior to turning over the solution to the customer and transitioning to operations.

Alpha testing describes acceptance testing done in a test environment within the development team, while beta testing is a field test where actual users operate the solution for a limited time period. During beta testing, information about defects and usage are collected. These are removed during the beta testing phase before the solution is finalized (the process of creating a final, shipped version is often called "going gold").

Acceptance Testing Effort

The amount of acceptance testing is based on risk. If the risk associated with failure during operations is high, then several days or weeks must be devoted to acceptance testing. If the risk of operational impact is low or patch updates can be rolled out frequently and automatically, then acceptance testing can be reduced.

Acceptance Criteria

To facilitate acceptance testing, each requirement, use case, or user story must have an associated set of minimal acceptance criteria. If those criteria are met, then the requirement is deemed to have passed acceptance testing. In the absence of well-defined acceptance criteria, there is often disagreement whether the requirement has been met or whether the requirement has been misunderstood.

Operational Acceptance Testing

In addition to acceptance by users and customers, system administrators and other IT support personnel must also test the solution to ensure that the solution can be installed and managed as planned. Testing may include disaster recovery testing, backup/restore testing, fail-over testing, user management testing, and other maintenance testing.

Regression Testing

Regression testing is done whenever a change to the solution has been made. A change could be the implementation of a new feature or an update to an existing feature. In an iterative project lifecycle, regression testing is done at the end of every iteration.

Regression testing involves re-running every test in the test suite to check that all functions still work as before. The goal of regression testing is to catch unintended side effect when the implementation is modified.

In order for regression testing to be feasible, automated testing tools are needed. Otherwise, the labor of re-running all tests in a test suite can quickly overwhelm the resources of a testing team.

Test Planning

The testing approaches used by a solution implementation team should be planned out in advance and documented so that there's agreement on the scope of testing and the associated effort.

Test planning and management will be addressed in more detail later. IEEE Standard 829-2008 is a valuable resource on how to write test plans.

Influence of Lifecycle

The project lifecycle or system development methodology used to manage the project impacts when and how testing is done.

A lifecycle methodology guides the team during the development of the system and prescribes activities and deliverables. Most organizations have their own internally developed methods that leverage industry best practices.

Project lifecycle methodologies can be broadly classified into two overall extremes: sequential and iterative methods.

Sequential

In the sequential or waterfall approach, development is done in distinct stages. It starts with planning, followed by requirements analysis, solution design, implementation, and finally testing. This approach is illustrated in Figure 4.

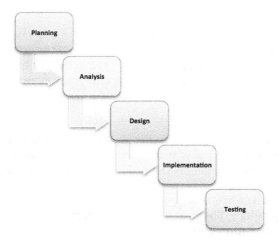

FIGURE 4. WATERFALL PROJECT LIFECYCLE

This approach is more traditional and is practiced generally by more established organizations. It is best when the requirements are well understood, are unlikely to change, and overall project risks are low. By its nature it is heavy on documentation and planning. The project phases are sequential and controlled. A transition to the next phase requires conclusion of the previous phase along with formal approval. Because of this "one-way" flow through the various phases it is often referred to as the "waterfall approach."

Component and integration testing is done continually by the developers, while system and acceptance testing are done at the end of development by a separate testing team.

Iterative/Agile

The more modern approach is to break the project into smaller phases called iterations. Each iteration lasts a relatively short amount of time (about 3-6 weeks), produces a deliverable that can be demonstrated and tested, is comprised of analysis, design, implementation, and testing, and adapts to the issues uncovered in the prior iteration. The approach is illustrated in Figure 5.

An iterative project team addresses the requirements with the highest risks early so that adjustments can be made if the risk materializes. They produce a testable (and potentially deployable) solution every two to three iterations to gain feedback from the users. The deployed iterations are called increments or releases.

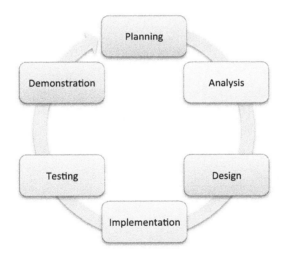

FIGURE 5. ITERATIVE/AGILE PROJECT LIFECYCLE

The developers do component testing during each iteration. Integration, system, and non-final acceptance testing is performed at the end of each iteration. Continuous testing and "releasability" is emphasized to drive engineering decisions.

This approach is preferable when requirements are likely to change or the project faces significant risks. The solution is implemented and released in increments and feedback is actively solicited at the end of every iteration.

Agile methods are a kind of iterative method; they are lighter on documentation and planning and rely on small co-located teams of skilled developers to increase productivity.

Most methodologies used in practice are somewhere between the extremes. Information Engineering is an example of a sequential methodology, while the Unified Process (UP), Scrum, and Extreme Programming (XP) are examples of iterative methodologies. Most organizations start with a commercial process purchased from a consulting organization that is then customized to their culture and environment.

Summary

- Testing is a risk-based activity that is limited implying that not all defects can be found
- Testing is an iterative and incremental endeavor
- Project lifecycles determine when, how, and to what extent testing is done
- Testing is done on the static code and the running solution
- User acceptance testing requires well-define acceptance criteria that must be defined when the requirements are documented

Service Testing Practices

Upon completion of this chapter you will be able to:

✓ Test the services or functions provided by a solution
✓ Reduce the number of test cases through equivalence partitioning
✓ Identify common problems through boundary analysis
✓ Map application states and state transitions
✓ Leverage use cases to build better test cases
✓ Use decision tables to understand expected responses
✓ Perform *ad-hoc* exploratory testing when specifications are unavailable

Motivation

Testing is not an *ad hoc* activity and does not simply mean that one "bangs against" a solution in order to break it. Rather, testing is a formal activity that is documented in detail. In fact, one of the most important skills of a successful tester is to be detail oriented and methodical. Of course, the degree of formality depends on the type of solution that is being tested and the consequence of latent defects.

This chapter shows how to test software with "blinders on", *i.e.*, the solution is treated as a "black box" or in some cases as a "grey box". While programming skills are not necessary to be an effective tester, some understanding of programming is helpful, particularly when it comes to understanding boundary value analysis.

Exploratory vs. Predictive Testing

Exploratory testing is a type of *ad hoc* approach where testers proceed without a specific test plan. This approach is used when there is an absence of a formal specification or defined requirements. It is also used during reverse engineering to learn about the solution's functionality and capabilities. During exploratory testing, it is advisable to treat the software as the specification.

The opposite of exploratory testing is predictive testing, where testing is done based on specific test cases derived from the requirements specification.

Writing Test Cases

A test case defines the expected outcome for a specific set of stimuli. All test cases combined make up a test suite. In practice, the terms test case and test scenario are used interchangeably.

Writing test cases presumes that there is a requirements specification. If there is no specification, then exploratory testing is called for.

Test-to-Pass vs. Test-to-Fail

Organizations approach testing from two different perspectives: test to pass versus test to fail. When testing to pass, the tester checks that the solution meets the stated requirements and that it does not break when used in accordance with the specification. However, in practice, solutions are pushed by their users – there are frequently used in ways other than what the designers intended. The alternative is test-to-fail, where the solution is pushed to the edge and is made to break – testers are forcing errors and are using the solution in ways that were not anticipated in the specification.

Of course, testers should start with the test-to-pass approach to make sure that the solution meets the specification and that there are no defects when used properly. Then testers should "exercise" the solution and see how it behaves when used outside the design boundaries.

Discussion Question

What would *test-to-pass* and *test-to-fail* mean for a computer that you are trying to purchase?

Test Case Template

Test cases should be properly documented and tracked, ideally in a database such as those provided by testing tools. Documented test cases are critical for logging purposes and to know what exactly has been tested. Of course, they are essential for regression testing. Every time some aspect of the solution has changed, all test cases testing potentially affected areas must be re-run.

The test case should define the precise inputs and expected outputs; it is a series of stimulus/response pairs.

A test case should minimally contain the following attributes:

Attribute	Description
Unique Test Case Identifier	A unique identifier for the test case
Date	Date on which test was conducted
Test Object	Code module, screen, web page under test
Use Case	Use case being tested

Requirements	Identifiers of requirements that are being tested
Test Condition(s)	Test scenarios being investigated
Script	Specific inputs, expected outputs, and actual results
Assessment	Assessment of the test case as Successful or Failed
Version	Version of test object
Configuration	Information about the test environment, including operating system versions
Notes	General notes

Once the test case has been executed it may result in defect submissions. Each discovered defect is recorded in a defect database.

Use Case Analysis

Use cases describe more specific usage scenarios, whereas test cases simply apply a set of inputs to a test object to observe its reaction. As such, use cases are more realistic since they test an actual use of the system.

Definition of Use Case and Actor

To define the requirements of a solution, we look to its users, the ones that are interested in using the solution for some specific purpose. These users have specific requirements that need to be captured and documented so that the builders of the product know what they should build. Products, whose features can be described with use cases range from software applications, information systems, web sites, and services to hardware devices and consumer goods.

The most common definition of a use case is that **a use case is an interaction that a prospective user has with a solution, such as a software application or web site**. The prospective user is referred to as the **actor**. Most actors are human users, but they can also be external systems. The key is that an actor is external, *i.e.*, it represents an outside stimulus.

Each use case represents a goal that the actor intends to achieve by using the solution. The notion that a use case represents a goal is very important. A use case is not simply a user interface interaction or a single functional requirement. It is a higher-level requirement that defines some need that some user has. This is the reason why use cases define *user requirements*.

Below are two examples of use cases for *BoatVentures*. The actors are in bold and the use case goal is underlined:

- The **broker** intends to capture a new charter lead

- The **charter guest** intends to <u>search for available yachts</u>

Use Case Diagram

During initial analysis and when talking with stakeholders, many analysts like to sketch the actors and the use cases on a whiteboard. A use case diagram provides a visualization of the actors and their initiated use cases. The use case diagram uses very simple symbols and does not contain much information. Most of the information on how the use case works is contained in the use case narrative (also often called the use case document or simply the use case.)

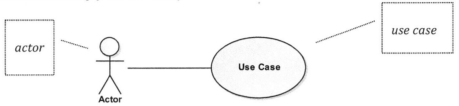

FIGURE 6. UML USE CASE DIAGRAM SYMBOLS

A use case diagram shows actors, use cases, and which actors participate in which use cases. When more advanced analysis is desired, the use case diagram can also show relationships between the use cases (inclusion, extension, generalization) and the actors (role map).

The name of the use case can be written inside the oval, underneath or even above the oval. Write the use case name below the use case oval when you sketch on a whiteboard. The actor icon is sometimes changed if the actor represents an external system rather than a human user

The use case diagram is a high-level UML diagram that summarizes the actors and the use cases in which they participate. The diagram is principally used to illustrate scope. The actual details of the use cases are contained in the narratives. Figure 6 shows the basic symbols of the UML use case diagram: the actor and the use case. An actual diagram would have several actors and numerous use cases. Larger diagrams are decomposed into several smaller diagrams for easier manageability.

Use Case Name

A use case defines a goal that an actor expects to achieve when interacting with our product. So when naming a use case it must start with a verb to indicate an action and then define the outcome. Examples of valid use case names are "capture new charter lead" and "view available yachts".

Use cases are often confused with detailed functional requirements, however, use cases are written at a higher level – they represent a *feature of the solution* rather than some detailed requirement that defines the features. For example, "record charter guest's credit card number" is not a use case; rather it is a detailed requirement for the use case

"Book Charter". It does not represent a goal in its own right, rather a step to achieving a goal of value.

Use Case Narrative

The details of each use case are documented in a narrative that:
- lists the steps in each successful and unsuccessful scenario that make up the interaction
- defines context
  - <u>pre-conditions</u>: set of conditions that must be true in order for the use case to be successful
  - <u>post-conditions</u>: set of conditions that will be true once the use case has completed either successfully or unsuccessfully
- links to detailed requirements and business rules
- links to process models, data models, user interface models, and other artifacts that support the use case

While the use cases are generally written for developers and to understand user needs, they are a great base for writing test cases.

Most organizations use a standard template for the use case narrative. Although tools exist for organizing use cases, most organizations prefer to use Microsoft Word. When using Word there are two general approaches for writing the documents: one document per use case or one document that contains all use cases. The document per use case strategy is often the simplest and makes the use cases more easily manageable.

Organizing use cases into packages makes the collection of use cases easier to manage. UML uses package diagrams to show the different collections of use cases. The grouping into packages is completely up to the analyst; they can use whatever grouping mechanism they prefer. Some like a package for each functional area (e.g., accounting, reporting, and administration), others like one package per release, or one package per actor. Packages are in fact a general UML mechanism for organizing modeling elements. Later we will see how they are used to organize class entities in a data model.

Title:	\<use case name/title\>	*Identifier:*	\<unique id\>
Description:	\<short description of the use case; often expressed as an agile user story\>		
Author:		*Version:*	*Priority:*
Perspective:	\<current or future state\>		*Type:*
Duration:		*Frequency:*	*Status:*

Pre Conditions:	• \<list of pre conditions\>
Scenarios:	• \<list of scenarios\>
Example Scenario:	\<narrative of an example\>
Normal Path:	\<list of steps in the normal path or the basic/normal scenario\>
Variations:	\<list of variations\>
Post Conditions:	\<list of post conditions\>
Related Requirements & Rules	\<list of related or applicable requirements and/or business rules\>
Open Issues & Notes:	\<any applicable notes, constraints, assumptions, or other information that can aid the implementer\>

Figure 7 below represent a typical use case template that can be adapted for the use case narrative. There are no standards to use case template and many organization and use case authoring tools have their own formats.

Title:	\<use case name/title\>	*Identifier*:	\<unique id\>
Description:	\<short description of the use case; often expressed as an agile user story\>		
Author:	*Version:*		*Priority:*
Perspective:	\<current or future state\>		*Type:*
Duration:	*Frequency*:		*Status*:
Pre Conditions:	• \<list of pre conditions\>		
Scenarios:	• \<list of scenarios\>		
Example Scenario:	\<narrative of an example\>		
Normal Path:	\<list of steps in the normal path or the basic/normal scenario\>		
Variations:	\<list of variations\>		

Post Conditions:	<list of post conditions>
Related Requirements & Rules	<list of related or applicable requirements and/or business rules>
Open Issues & Notes:	<any applicable notes, constraints, assumptions, or other information that can aid the implementer>

FIGURE 7. USE CASE NARRATIVE TEMPLATE

Figure 8 shows an example of a completed use case narrative template for the use case "View Available Yachts".

Title:	View Available Yachts		*Identifier:*	UC003	
Description:	The agent views a list of yachts that meet specified preferences.				
Author:	MI	*Version:* 1.0		*Priority:*	2
Perspective:	O *Current State* ⊙ *Future State*			*Type:*	System
Duration:	Minutes	*Frequency:* Daily		*Status:*	Approved
Pre Conditions:	• Yachts are in the inventory				
Scenarios:	• Successful viewing of yachts • No yachts meet the specified preferences • No yachts in inventory				
Example Scenario:	Rick Tierney, a charter agent with *BoatVentures*, gets a call from a potential charter client who wants to know if they have a sport fishing boat that can accommodate him and his four business associates for a half day of near shore fishing.				
Normal Path:	1. This use case starts when the need for a particular yacht arises 2. The system asks the agent to provide the specifications for the yacht 3. The system asks the agent to provide the charter date {V1} 4. The system displays the available yachts matching the specifications for the provided dates along with their daily charter fees 5. The system produces a document in PDF format containing the list of the available yachts along with their amenities, crewing requirements, and all costs 6. The broker specifies the guest's profile or enters an e-mail address if no profile has been created {V2}				

7. This use case ends when a list of available yachts with costs has been sent to the guest as an attachment to an e-mail message {*V2*}

Variations:	**V1**: **No Dates Provided**

1. The system displays all yachts
2. Use case continues

V2: **No E-Mail Address Available**

1. The system displays all yachts
2. Use case continues

Post Conditions:	• The yachts matching the specifications are listed
	• An e-mail with an attachment has been sent to the guest

Related Requirements & Rules	None

Open Issues & Notes:	If the guest does not have an e-mail address or does not provide one, then the agent reads the available yachts displayed on the screen to the guest

FIGURE 8. SAMPLE USE CASE NARRATIVE

Scenarios and Use Cases

Use cases are analyzed and defined fully through scenarios. Each scenario is a path through the use case. There are three kinds of scenarios: normal, alternate, and exception.

Normal Scenario

The normal scenario is the normal or basic path and is analyzed first. It defines the system interaction under normal circumstances. There is only one normal scenario per use case.

The analyst starts by eliciting the normal scenario first. Then each step in the basic path is evaluated in collaboration with the subject matter experts and users. At each step, ask:

- Are there other ways in which this step can be completed?
- What could happen here?
- How might this be done differently?
- Does it always happen like that?
- What should we do if it happens differently?
- Is the outcome always the same? When is it different?
- Can we assume that the inputs are always as expected?

Document each variation (an alternate or exception scenario) separately. For each scenario, state the trigger that causes it to happen, *e.g.*, *No Matching Yachts Found*.

The normal scenario is also often referred to as the basic path, basic scenario, happy path, sunny day scenario, the typical course of events, or usual scenario.

Alternate Scenario

An alternate scenario is a variation of the normal path but still results in a successful outcome of the use case; it is a variation of the normal path. Unlike the normal scenario, there can be multiple alternate scenarios.

Exception Scenario

An exception scenario describes a failed interaction where something does not go as expected and results in a failed outcome for the use case.

Exception and alternate scenarios are collectively referred to as variations, subflows, or variant scenarios.

Scenario Writing Best Practices

A use case scenario should start with the key phrase: *"This use case starts when …"* and should clearly state the trigger for the use case.

A scenario trace is a list of the steps or activities that are being performed by the actor and the system to achieve the use case goal. In the basic path there are no if statements, exceptions, or other flow controls.

The scenario traces should not contain any user interface specifications, such as "the user presses TAB to advance to the next field". Any such user interface requirements should be stated separately in the storyboard to which the narrative links.

Write each scenario statement using this format:

> The <**actor or system**> <*verb*> <object(s)>.

For example: The **system** *records* the payment. Objects should be underlined. Later, the objects will be defined in more detail in a data model and visualized in a conceptual UML class diagram.

Use Case Context

It is important to define the boundaries of the use case, *i.e.*, what do we assume will have happened before and what will be the (testable) outcome of the use case.

The post-conditions are particularly important for testing. If the post-conditions are achieved we can conclude that the use case completed successfully.

Aside from the post-conditions for the basic path, you also need to define the post-conditions to every other scenario regardless whether it is successful or not. After all, an unsuccessful scenario might still have testable post-conditions.

Linking to Detailed Requirements

The narrative steps cannot document the full detail that is needed for implementation. Therefore, link each step to detailed functional requirements and applicable business rules. The requirements and rules are cataloged separately in a requirements catalog and a business rules catalog.

Each requirement in the catalog should be uniquely numbered, defined, documented, and explained.

Requirements and Rules Catalogs

The detailed functional requirements as well as all non-functional (quality of service) requirements are cataloged in a list, such as a table or in a requirements management tool. The same is true for business rules. See the Cast Study requirements specification for an example on how to link use cases to requirements and business rules.

Documenting Variations

Variations are exception or alternate scenarios and should be documented separately from the normal scenario, *i.e.*, the basic path.

Each variation is identified through a sequentially assigned identifier, *e.g.*, V2. When a step has a variation, the variation identifier is listed as part of the step.

For example, step 6 in the basic path has an exception: what if no e-mail address is available? The variations are documented separately so as to not pollute the basic path scenario:

Visualizing Use Cases

Use case narratives can be difficult to decipher by programmers and subject matter experts, particularly if there are many variations. The analyst should create graphical visualizations of the use case by creating a process model.

Several visual languages for modeling processes have been developed:

- UML Activity Diagram
- Business Process Modeling Notation
- Flow Chart

Creating Test Cases

When testing solutions, there are often thousand or more possible scenarios to test. Use Case Scenario Analysis, Equivalence Class Partitioning, Boundary Value Analysis, Decision Tables, and State Charting can help reduce the number of test cases and focus on the most important ones. Use these techniques to help define the right test scenarios.

Use Case Analysis

Each scenario of each use case becomes the basis for a test case. Since use cases are devoid of implementation details, they have to be expanded before they can become fully specified test cases.

Equivalence Class Partitioning

Equivalence partitioning is a methodical approach to reducing the number (often infinite) of possible test cases into a smaller, more manageable, but still effective set of test cases. This technique is also often called equivalence partitioning or equivalence classing.

> **Definition**
>
> An equivalence class or partition is a set of test cases that exercise the same part of the solution and therefore reveal the same defect if there is one present.

An equivalence partition (equivalence class) is a set of data values that presumably are handled the same way by the solution. Therefore, instead of testing all possible inputs, only one representative input value is tested. If the test passes for the sample, then it is assumed to also handle all other values in the equivalence partition. Equivalence partition should be defined for correct as well as incorrect input values. Of course, this presumes that the equivalence partitions were developed correctly.

Example

Let's take an example from the *BoatVentures* case. When booking a charter, guests have to provide the number of days for which they would like to charter a yacht. In this situation any value greater than zero is valid, while any value of zero or less is invalid. Testing all possible scenarios is impossible as there are an infinite number. So, what is the practical set of test cases?

Let's break it up first into two partitions: valid versus invalid. Anything above zero in valid. If there were no defined upper value for a charter term than taking a very large value would be an appropriate representative. Let's choose 10 as the valid representative. Since anything zero or less is invalid, taking 0 would be a good choice. With that we have reduced the infinite number of test cases to just two: test for 10 days (valid) and for 0 days (invalid).

Boundary Value Analysis

Not all values are equally likely to fail, as programmers tend to make more mistakes at the "boundaries" of equivalence partitions. This has to do with the fact that programmers frequently program control logic statements, such as IF or SWITCH, incorrectly. For example, if *BoatVentures* states that yacht charters over 7 days receive a 10% discount, then we would expect that there is a control flow statement in the code that tests for that condition. The statement may look somewhat like the one below:

```
if (Booking.Days > 7)

    Booking.Price *= 0.1;
```

However, programmers may have interpreted or misread the "over 7" condition and may have code it as ">= 7" or perhaps even "== 7". So, test cases should be created for each equivalence class around the boundary since most errors occur right around the boundary. Always test at the boundary, and one below and one above the boundary. So, in this case there would be three equivalence classes leading to three test cases, 7 booking days, 6 booking days, and 8 booking days.

Boundary conditions also occur with counters, looping or iterations over collections. Any time, there is some kind of "edge" then a boundary condition can occur.

Boundary Value Analysis attempts to identify boundary conditions and create test cases based on them.

Identifying Boundary Edges

When defining equivalence classes, rather than taking random values, it is most revealing to choose values at the boundary edges where programmers are most likely to make mistakes. When a boundary condition has been identified, create an equivalence class for a value just inside the boundary, the last valid data point, and an invalid data point just outside the boundary. Table 4 summarizes the most common boundary value analysis rules.

TABLE 4. BOUNDARY VALUE ANALYSIS RULES

Scenario	Equivalence Classes	Example

Input value in a specific range from a minimum to a maximum value	• Create two equivalence classes for valid values, one at either extreme
	• Create two equivalence classes for invalid values, one just below the minimum an one just above the maximum
		"A bare-boat charter must be between 1 and 21 days."
		
		Valid Data:
		  • Test 1 and 21
		Invalid Data:
		  • Test 0 and 22

Input value in a specific range that is subdivided	• Create two equivalence classes for valid values, one at either extreme • Create two equivalence classes for invalid values, one just below the minimum an one just above the maximum • Create three equivalence classes for valid value, one at the condition point, one just above (or below), and one just below the end of the range	"The maximum length of a crewed charter is 14 days, but a surcharge of $500 is applied for charters of 7 days or more." Valid Data: • Test 1 and 14 • Test 7 and 8 Invalid Data: • Test 0 and 15 • Test 6
Input value from a set of pre-defined values that are all treated the same way	• Create an equivalence test for any valid value from the set • Create an equivalence class for any value not in the set	*"The port of embarkation must be either Falmouth, Oak Bluffs, or Vineyard Haven."* Valid Data: • Test "Falmouth" Invalid Data: • Test "Woods Hole"
Input value from a set of pre-defined values where each is treated differently	• Create an equivalence test for all valid values from the set • Create an equivalence class for any value not in the set	*"The cost of the charter is dependent on the port of embarkation."* Valid Data: • Test "Falmouth", "Oak Bluffs", and "Vineyard Haven" Invalid Data: • Test "Woods Hole"
An output is dependent on a binary condition	• Create an equivalence test for where the condition is met • Create an equivalence class where the condition is not met	*"The operator of a bare-boat charter must have a valid USCG License."* Valid Data: • Test for an operator with a valid license Invalid Data: • Test for an operator without a license or with an invalid license

Managing Combinatorial Explosion

To reduce the number of test cases, a test designer should combine as many equivalence classes for valid inputs. However, equivalence classes for invalid inputs may not be combined so that defects can be clearly isolated and traced.

In computer software, many fields have a maximum length that is a power of 2. So testing powers of 2 is also often helpful. For example, text fields often have a maximum length that is a power of 2, *e.g.*, 16, 32, 64, 128, 256, or 1024. Test at and one above each of those boundaries. This is particularly helpful for exploratory testing.

Default and Empty Values

Another common source of coding errors concern default, empty, blank, null, zero, or unspecified values. For example, a text entry field may be left empty a numeric input field could be left blank. A query from a database could result in an empty (or null) result set. Users may forget to fill in fields and be content with the default value – is the default value valid in all cases?

Bad Data

The equivalence classes defined thus far are intended for *test-to-pass* test cases. In practice, users may be careless or misguided in providing input values. For example, they may provide a numeric input when text is required or otherwise provide bad, incorrect, invalid, or garbage data. Therefore, test designers must create *test-to-fail* test cases. Bad data should be its own equivalence class. Table 5 summarizes some of the most common invalid data test cases to consider.

TABLE 5. INVALID INPUT DATA EQUIVALENCE CLASSES

Input Field Type	Possible Invalid Data
Text field	<ul><li>Numeric only value</li><li>Empty or blank field</li><li>Leading space(s)</li><li>Only spaces</li><li>Embedded Quotes (" or ')</li><li>Embedded special characters ($, %, &, <, >, @)</li><li>Very large strings (over 256 characters)</li></ul>
Numeric field	<ul><li>Text values</li><li>Empty or blank field</li><li>Leading space(s)</li><li>Only spaces</li><li>Embedded commas</li><li>Fractional values, e.g., 1.76</li><li>Very small and very large values</li></ul>

Currency field	• Text values • Empty or blank field • Leading space(s) • Only spaces • Embedded commas • Fractional values, e.g., 1.76 • Very small and very large values • Embedded currency symbols, e.g., $ or €
Date field	• Dates in the past • Dates very far in the future • Different date formatting, e.g., MM/DD/YY or DD.MM.YY • Two versus four digit years • Illegal month or day values, e.g., 14 for month or 32 for day • Blank field • Unusual separators (. / - | # *)
Credit card field	• Empty or blank field • 15 vs 16 digits credit card numbers • Leading digit that conflicts with card type, e.g., 5 for a Visa • Incorrect security code • Spaces in card number • Leading spaces

Testing-to-fail is more exploratory in nature and relies more on the intuition of the tester. Therefore, testers should try things that normal users might not do, i.e., try to break the software, try unusual inputs, be mischievous.

Decision Tables

Decision tables provide a methodical way to describe complex business rules where an outcome is based on multiple conditions and simple boundary analysis won't suffice.

A decision table is a tabular representation containing an exhaustive list of all conditions that affect some action, outcome, or calculation. The table can be arranged vertically or horizontally. A decision table provides for an accounting of all combinations of factors. It helps define a complete set of test cases and ensures that all scenarios are considered. They are ideal when multiple factors can occur simultaneously.

The decision table is a common documentation strategy used by test designers when documenting complex conditional rules:

• easier to visualize combinations of factors
• compact presentation of factors

- easier to spot mistakes and omissions
- groups related rules into a single representational structure
- translatable into a system executable form

Figure 9 below shows an example of a decision table summarizing rules regarding pricing discounts available for charters at *BoatVentures*. Here are the rules encoded in the table:

- *If the charter is longer than 4 hours, then a 10% discount is applied*
- *Parties of fewer than 3 guests do not require a mate and are discounted 5%*
- *All off-season charters receive a 10% discount*
- *All discounts are cumulative and multiple discounts can apply*

	Possible Test Scenarios							
	1	2	3	4	5	6	7	8
Longer than 4 hours?	Y	Y	Y	Y	N	N	N	N
2 or fewer guests?	Y	Y	N	N	Y	Y	N	N
Off-season booking?	Y	N	Y	N	Y	N	Y	N
Discount %	25%	15%	20%	10%	15%	5%	10%	-

(Factors: Longer than 4 hours?, 2 or fewer guests?, Off-season booking?; Outcome: Discount %)

FIGURE 9. DECISION TABLE

To summary, a decision table is a matrix representation of the complete set mutually exclusive conditional factors for some related set of rules. Each column in the decision table becomes a test case.

Constructing a Decision Table

Start by defining the conditions or factors that determine the actions. Each condition must contain a subject, domain, and states. Next, define a list of possible actions. Formally, a decision table is a relation that maps conditions to actions.

For each condition determine number of possibilities (n), which can be binary (yes/no, true/false) or higher order. Then calculate the product of each condition's possibility cardinality to arrive at the total number of conditions. Write the conditions as columns in the decision table and number them from 1 to *X*.

So, if you have three factors as in Figure 9 you would have three binary (yes/no) factors. Each has two possible outcomes and therefore there are 2*2*2 = 8 possible combinations of conditions. Next, eliminate illegal combinations and then populate the table. Meet with the subject matter experts and complete the actions for each combination of factors. If you have too many conditions, write several tables to simplify each table.

Figure 10 lists the steps involved in constructing a decision table.

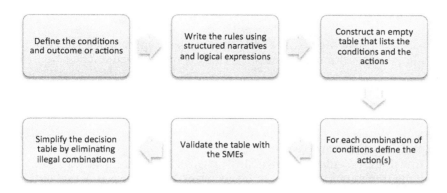

FIGURE 10. DECISION TABLE CONSTRUCTION STEPS

State Charting

The testing to this point has concentrated on test cases based on various inputs – both valid and invalid. However, the logic and control flow in the solution has not yet been validated. State charting helps in testing the different solution states and whether the solution progresses through the states in the expected sequence.

State charts are generally developed during static testing and design reviews and should be available before testing starts. During exploratory testing, state charts are useful when exploring the different application areas and functions.

UML State Chart Diagram

While there are several state charting notations, UML state charts are a worldwide standard for analysis and design modeling. The basic UML state chart symbols are shown in Figure 11 below.

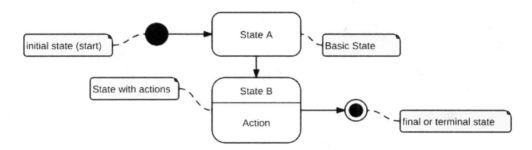

FIGURE 11. UML STATE CHART DIAGRAM SYMBOLS

State charts can be used to model overall application states as well as intra-use case states.

Navigation Charts

Each screen or page can be viewed as a valid state and getting from one screen or page to another would be a transition. Such as state chart is often called a navigation chart or dialog map.

Creating a navigation chart involves four steps:

1. Uniquely name each screen or page with an identifier (*e.g.*, SC001 or PG-01)
2. Create a state for each screen or page
3. Use transitions to indicate navigability between screens or pages
4. Label the transitions with the command, event, trigger, or action that initiates the navigation (*e.g.*, Press "Home")

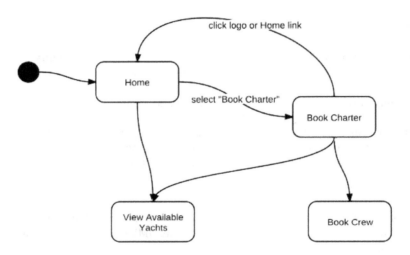

FIGURE 12. NAVIGATION CHART

Application Mode Maps

Mode maps are applied when an application enters some processing phase where different actions are valid depending on the mode of the interaction. A state chart can help map out the different modes and valid actions.

For example, when entering a time charter only up to six guests are allowed to be carried on the vessel. On the other hand, a demise charter can carry up to twelve guests but requires crew that is booked separately from the charter. In addition, a surcharge is applied. Any charter with more than 12 guests is not allowed according to USCG rules. In this case the "mode flag" is the charter type: *time* versus *demise* versus *invalid*. Depending on the charter "mode" different rules apply.

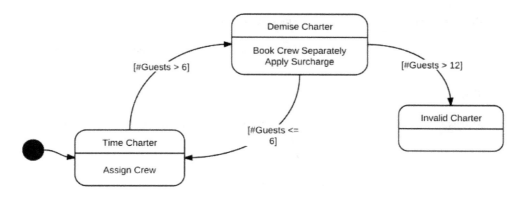

FIGURE 13. APPLICATION MODE MAP

Recording Defects

Defects discovered during testing must be recorded and details of the test and the unexpected result must be communicated to the solution development team. The report must include sufficient information for the solution team to understand the defect and be able to replicate it. It is expected that supporting documentation such as screen shots or narrated screen casts are included in the report. Tools such as *SnagIt, Snipping Tool*, or other screen capturing tools are often used to produce screen shots. Screen casting tools capture entire interactions as a replayable video. Tools such as screenr.com, *JingIt, ComStudio, Camtasia, iMovie,* or *Hypercam* are useful for this purpose.

Defect Attributes

A defect report (also often called a bug or incident report) should minimally contain the information shown in Table 6:

TABLE 6. ELEMENTS OF A DEFECT REPORT

Attribute	Description
Unique Defect Identifier	A unique identifier for the defect
Detailed Description of Defect	A detailed description of the defect that contains enough information for developers to understand the nature of the defect and to replicate it
Solution Version & Module	The version of the solution or application in which the defect is manifested plus the module or page in which the defect is present or was discovered
Script	A detailed list of the steps with screen shots that shows how the defect was triggered

Date Discovered	The date on which the defect was first discovered
Source	The person, customer, or user who first reported the defect
Tester	The tester who reproduced and recorded the defect
Status	The current status of the defect. One of Open, Closed, Non-Reproducible, Assigned, Deferred, Resolved, Repaired
Date Closed	The date on which the defects was resolved
Severity	The severity of the defect describing its impact on the viability of the solution
Priority	The priority of the defect assessing its urgency for repair
Type of Defect	The type of the defect

Summary

- Testing is a methodical activity that requires careful analysis
- Test cases are either *test-to-pass* or *test-to-fail*
- Use cases help in defining test cases; there is one test case for each use case scenario
- Equivalence partitioning reduces the number of test cases
- Boundary value analysis helps define the right equivalence classes
- Decision tables exhaustively list all combination of factors that affect an outcome when testing complex business rules
- State chart help analyze and track the mode of an application
- Defects are carefully recorded following a template that contains the information needed to reproduce and resolve the error

Quality of Service Testing Practices

Upon completion of this chapter you will be able to:

✓   Establish performance characteristics of solutions
✓   Evaluate the usability, security, and recoverability of a solution

Motivation

The testing conducted thus far has focused on testing the services or functions implemented by the solution and to determine if they meet the specified requirements. Quality of service testing, on the other hand, does not look for defects, but rather how well the solution will function in an actual setting.

Performance Testing

Performance testing includes response time testing as well as load testing and stress testing.

Load testing helps establish the maximum operating performance of an application through empirical measurements, while response time testing seeks to establish the average response time of an application. Response times can often be measured through manual timers, while load testing requires the use of specialized tools and protocols.

In short, performance testing is the overall process, while response time testing establishes the performance in a single-user environment, while load testing evaluates performance in expected conditions. Stress testing tries to break the solution by applying extreme loads.

Response Time Testing

Common performance metrics relating to response time that should be collected and reported include:

- System response times
- End-to-end task completion times for use cases

For each of the above metrics, descriptive statistics including number of samples, minimum, maximum, average, standard deviation, and various percentiles should be reported. When possible, graphs and charts should be created to aid in communication of the results.

The results should be written up in a report (document or wiki are acceptable). The report should include the raw data as well as summary charts and graphs. It should also state details about the testing methodology and environment. It is also important to perform the tests in a stand-alone single-user environment and a multi-user environment. Response time testing is generally done under normal loads rather than the extreme loads of stress testing.

Load Testing

Load testing verifies that the solution functions under various operational conditions, such as number of concurrent users, number of concurrent transactions, or number of incoming HTTP requests.

Stress Testing

Stress testing is a type of performance test that focuses on evaluating a solution's robustness, availability, and reliability under extreme conditions, such as very large number of simultaneous users or concurrent transactions running on an overloaded server with limited memory and limited storage space. The goal is to determine if the solution can handle peak usage periods.

Tools

Stress testing and load testing generally require a load generator that simulates a large number of users or transactions. Manual testing is typically not practical.

For more information on guidelines for performance and load testing, consult (Meier, Farre, Bansode, Barber, & Rea, 2007)[3].

Security Testing

Security testing is performed to evaluate whether the application and its information are kept from unauthorized use. Security testing involves:

- **Authentication**: Is the person who they claim they are? This is commonly accomplished through user names and passwords, although biometrics is used more often. Check that passwords are kept secure and that they are not easy to guess. Change password frequently, but don't make the policy so difficult that users resort to writing their passwords down to remember.
- **Authorization**: Does the user have access to this function? This is commonly done through access control lists and groups. Check that features are only accessible to those users that have access.

---

[3] An electronic copy of this book is available at http://msdn.microsoft.com/en-us/library/bb924375.aspx.

- **Confidentiality**. Is information kept from unauthorized parties? This includes encryption of stored and transmitted information, as well as policies for handling printed information. Pay particular attention to network transmission of data (*http* vs *https* on the web, for example) and display of confidential information on screens. Also watch for cookies or plain files, as well as information stored within HTML pages or XML documents.
- **Integrity**. Has the information been altered? When information is stored or transmitted there is the possibility that is has been intercepted and perhaps altered. Use checksums and encryption to dissuade alteration.
- **Non-Repudiation**. Is the sender who it says it is? This is commonly implemented through digital certificates and assures that the sender of the message is whom the receiver believes it is and the sender knows that the right receiver has gotten the message.

Usability Testing

Software solutions are meant to be used by people and therefore understanding how humans interact with software applications is important. Usability testing evaluates how easily users can achieve their goals when interacting with a software application. For example, how easy is it for a charter broker to view all available yachts that might meet a client's needs or how easily can a client book a charter through a web form?

Usability testing does not point out the same kinds of defects that service-level functional testing does – we are not looking to see if the solution's features conform to the specification. Rather, a tester evaluates how well the user can achieve his or her goals. Usability evaluates how quickly a user can finish a task, how many errors the user makes, and how satisfied the user is with the interaction.

Usability testing primarily concentrates on the user interface: the windows, menus, icons, dialogs, pages, screens, forms, and so forth. However, some solutions may include printed forms, voice interfaces, or mobile computing devices. In those cases, usability testing extends beyond the user interface.

It is important to recognize that usability testing is a specialty of its own. User Interaction Designers and User Experience Designers are trained to evaluate usability and their advice and expertise should be used in usability testing. However, there are situations where a tester and quality assurance specialist are the only available resources and therefore they need to know the basics of usability testing.

Usability Measures

In general, usability captures how easily and quickly users can learn how to navigate a user interface or website to achieve their goals and how satisfied they are with that process. Overall, usability measures the quality of a user's interactive experience. Usability evaluations are focused on the following metrics:

- How quickly can a user learn to navigate the user interface and carry out a task even if they have never seen the interface before?

- How well does a user recall what he or she has learned from previous interactions?
- How fast can a user complete a specific task and is that the most efficient way to doing it, *i.e.*, are their simpler designs?
- How many mistakes does the user makes and how easily can the user recover from those errors? Does an error preclude the user from achieving their goal?
- How satisfied is the user with the interactive experience, *i.e.*, how much do they "like" the product?

Usability Studies

Usability is measured in different ways. Most usability studies involve users trying a product and then completing a survey or participating in a focus group. Using software such as keystroke loggers, testers can measure how quickly a user accomplishes a task or how many errors they make. Devices such as eye gaze trackers[4] can help testers determine where a user focuses when interacting with an interface.

Nielsen (Nielsen, 2000) showed that the number of usability issues k found in a usability study with n users is approximated by the formula:

$$k = N(1 - (1 - L)^n)$$

where N is the total number of usability issues concealed in the design and L is the proportion of usability problem discovered through a single-user test. Studies by Nielsen and others suggest an average value of $L = 0.31$ (or 31%). A graph showing the number of usability issues discovered as the number of users rises in provided in Figure 14.

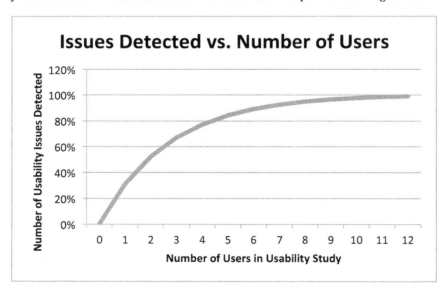

FIGURE 14. RETURN ON USABILITY TESTING

---

[4] GazeHawk (www.gazehawk.com) is an online usability service for generating "heat maps" of web sites.

Not surprisingly, not conducting any usability tests does not reveal any issues. However, what is interesting about Nielsen's research is that working with only 5 users will give you about 80% of issues. Furthermore, you get about 99% of the problems with only about 12-15 users. So, in practice, even if a usability study only involves 5 to 6 users, you will get the majority of the usability problems.

Best Practices in Usability

The most important characteristics of good user interfaces regardless of platform or operating system include:

- Consistent with usability standards and guidelines
    - Does the interface follow accepted styles and guidelines, such as Shneiderman's 8 Golden Rules or the Hix/Hartson Guidelines?
    - Does the interface follow platform style guides, such as those for iOS or Windows?
- Intuitive to use even for novice users
    - Can novice users use the software without training?
    - Does the interface follow an easily recognizable metaphor?
- Consistent presentation
    - Are dialog, messages, menus, and other interface controls consistent?
- Customizable controls to suit specific needs
    - Can the interface be customized or personalized?
    - What about language localization?
- Ample feedback regarding progress and status
    - Is there sufficient feedback on progress of activities?
    - Are there progress bars, status messages, and other feedback devices?
- Simplicity and minimalism in design
    - Does the interface use the least number of steps to accomplish action?
    - Are controls large enough to click without error?
- Accessible to all users including those with impairments
    - Are font sizes adjustable?
    - Does the interface only rely on color?
    - Is feedback only done with sound?
    - What about users with kinesthetic impairments? What if they can't use a mouse or select a small target on a touch screen?

There are a number of good resources for usability testing and overall usability design, including www.usability.gov and www.useIT.com. The www.usability.gov website is particularly helpful; it contains many template, samples, guidelines, checklists, and best practices and is an invaluable resource for usability testing and design.

Recovery Testing

Systems can fail and organizations that have stringent "uptime" requirements or are perhaps contractually bound to a certain level of service generally employ "fail-over" mechanisms. There are several fail-over mechanisms that exist and must be tested to make sure they actually work:

67

- **Cold Spare**: A backup computer that is identical to the operational environment is available but will first have to be configured with the latest operational backups.
- **Hot Spare**: A backup computer that is kept synchronized with the operational computer and can be made operational in short time should the main computer fail.
- **Automatic Fail-Over**: An automatic system where a spare detects the failure of the main and automatically takes over.

Other items that should be checked as part of recovery testing are backups. Can the system be restored from backups? Does the backup process work? Are backup media retrievable? How long does that take? Is the right software and hardware available?

Also check network recovery, power recovery, and hardware failure recovery.

Summary

- Performance testing evaluates the response time under single-user loads, while load testing checks response time under multiple users; stress testing checks extreme conditions
- Usability testing evaluates how well the solution meets the needs of users and how easy it is for them to achieve their goals
- Security testing checks that information and functionality is not accessible to unauthorized parties
- Recover testing ensures that the solution can be recovered from a failure

Testing Web Applications

Upon completion of this chapter you will be able to:

- ✓ Apply basic black-box testing to web applications
- ✓ Assess the usability of web applications
- ✓ Understand which parts of a web application require testing
- ✓ Perform compatibility testing of web applications

Motivation

This chapter takes a look at special techniques and practices for testing web sites and web applications. While all of the previous techniques apply as well, there are some special considerations when testing web applications. While this chapter is principally geared to web application testing, the same practices apply to testing web sites.

Web Fundamentals

Web sites are created using a combination of HTML, JavaScript, and CSS. Web applications generally add interactive forms, XML, AJAX, and other embedded technologies to increase the fidelity of the interaction. Going forward, we will only use the term web application.

Web applications contain text (the layout of which is expressed in HTML and CSS), graphics (images, animation, and videos), hyperlinks, forms, and fields. Pages also contain embedded JavaScript performing hidden formatting, encoding, and processing. In addition, meta-tags contain hidden tagging and other information that can affect the display of the page.

The most difficult aspect of testing web applications is that the layout of a page is controlled by the browser and not by the programmer. Screen size, screen orientation, font sizes, and user customizations significantly affect the display of the page. Consider in particular the reduced screen sizes of mobile devices, such as tablets and smart phones or the reduced screen resolution of older computers and browsers embedded in game consoles.

Security is handled partly by the browser as well as the web server serving the web application's pages.

Testing Functionality

Testing web applications is a principally a black-box testing effort. Each page is treated as a block box.

Links

One of the most important aspects the web is the ability to link pages. Linked pages can be internal or external to the web site. Broken links are a common defect. Also look for *orphan pages* – pages that are in the web application but cannot be accessed, as there are no links to them. This requires a list of pages from the developers coupled with a site map.

Usability Aspects

Note that links can be embedded in text, graphics, and image maps. From a usability perspective make sure that hyperlinks are distinguishable from non-clickable text. It should be obvious to users that some area of the page is "clickable".

If an image is used as a link, make sure that it is "big enough" to be selectable, particularly on mobile browser. Consider in particular the reduced screen sizes of mobile devices, such as tablets and smart phones or the reduced screen resolution of older computers and browsers embedded in game consoles.

Creating a Site Map

Using state charts, create a site map that lists each page in the web application and all outgoing links. Draw a connection between the source page and its destination page. If the destination page is external to the application, add a new page to the state chart.

Forms

Forms provide a way for users to enter information. They consist of text boxes, text fields, list boxes, radio boxes, and check boxes. Figure 15 contains a sample form with text fields and a text box, along with a Submit and Reset button.

Forms fields should be tested like any other application. Boundary value analysis, decision tables, and equivalence class partitioning are particularly useful techniques. Also check empty form submissions and form reset. Assess formats for dates, times, credit card numbers, phone numbers, addresses, and names.

Contact Cathris

Your name: [   ]

Your email address: [   ]

Your phone number: [   ]

Details: [   ]
                               [   ]
                               [   ]

[Submit]   [Reset]

FIGURE 15. WEB FORM

Usability

When an error occurs, the feedback should be instructive and tell the user what is wrong and which field contain the offense. Instructions should be provided on how to fix the error.

Graphics

Graphics are embedded in a page as URL references which can be broken. Check that all images and videos load. If an image or video does not load, a placeholder "error image" will appear. See Figure 16 for an example. The actual "error image" or error message is browser dependent.

Cathris Logo

FIGURE 16. ERROR IMAGE FOR NON-LOADABLE GRAPHIC

Usability

Graphics should be easily readable on all screen sizes. Be particularly mindful of low-resolution devices such as smartphones, tablets, and kiosks.

Performance

Graphics images can be very large. The browser, not the web server, does the actual scaling. For example, embedding a 2048x1900 high resolution photo in a web page which scales the image to 256x198 would mean that the entire image's 3.8MB of data would need to be transmitted over the network from the web server to the web browser. The browser would then scale the image down to a paltry 4.9KB. Why transmit the data if it's not used? Programmers should compress images to the correct size before uploading it to the web site.

Be mindful of slow dialup or wireless connections. Mobile devices not only have potentially slow network connections with limited bandwidth but the bandwidth may be metered. Therefore, downloading unnecessarily large images or videos that are then scaled down before display may be very costly.

Most wireless as well as home cable networks are shared and the limited bandwidth should be used judiciously.

Color

Check that all colors display on the target device. Particularly check the default colors for hyperlinks. Consider the needs to older and colorblind users.

Fonts

Check that all fonts display correctly on the target device. Note that not all fonts work on all platforms. Browsers will substitute comparable fonts but that may adversely affect the page layout. Users can adjust the size of fonts as a browser option. Be particularly mindful of the needs of older users or those with vision impairment.

Testing Browser Compatibility

Check web pages on all target browsers, screen resolutions, and screen orientations. Note that tablets and smartphones can rotate their displays.

Be particularly aware of different browsers and different versions of those browsers. Also, check them on different operating systems; there are differences! Table 7 has a partial list of the most common browsers and the platforms on which they run.

TABLE 7. BROWSERS BY PLATFORM

Operating System/Platform	Browsers
Windows	Internet Explorer
	Firefox
	Chrome
	Safari
	Opera
	AOL
	Netscape
Mac OS X	Safari
	Firefox
	Chrome
Linux	Firefox
	Chrome
	Konqueror

Tablets	Opera
	Safari and Atomic on iPad
	Silk on Kindle Fire
	Chrome on Android
Smartphone	iPhone
	Android
	Blackberry
	Windows Phone
ChromeBook	Chrome on ChromeOS

Plug-Ins

If the web applications relies on plug-ins, be sure that they are available on all target platforms and either are loaded or can be loaded easily. Plug-ins are required for viewing PDF, Word document, Excel workbooks, and videos. Web applications may also contain Java applets or Flash animations, both of which require plug-ins.

While most of these plug-ins are installed by default on most operating systems, they may not be available on some. For example, *ChromeOS* does not support *Java*, while Safari on *iOS* (the operating system for *iPhone* and iPad) does not support *Flash*. Viewing *Word* or *Excel* documents may not be feasible on mobile devices.

Cookies

Many web applications use cookies to store temporary state data that is used to preserve information between sessions. Cookies may store private information as plain text. Be sure to determine if any cookies are used and what information is stored in the cookies.

If cookies are required by the application to track state, then cookies must be turned on in the browser. Users can disable that functionality which may lead to defects.

Evaluating Usability

For web applications to be useful, they must be usable. Usability means that the web pages are easy to navigate, that users know where they are, and that tasks are easy to perform. The web site should respond quickly and should be aesthetically pleasing. Be particularly mindful of older users and those with hearing, vision, or kinesthetic impairments.

Keep web page clutter-free with lots of white space. Make them easy to read. The table below summarizes Nielsen's *Top Mistakes in Web Design*[5]:

- **Frames**: Frames should be avoided. Instead use AJAX or other JavaScript based techniques to increase page fidelity.

---

[5] From Jacob Nielsen's web *http://www.useit.com/alertbox/990502.html*

- **Bleeding-Edge Technology**: Avoid using the latest and greatest technology. Focus on what works and what has the broadest browser support. Users should not have to hunt down the latest plug-in to view a page or document.
- **Scrolling Text**: Avoid scrolling text as it is hard to read and can be very distracting.
- **Animation Loops**: Avoid animated logos or other animation loops. They can be very distracting and may distract focus from more important part of your page.
- **Complex URLs**: Avoid complex URL or provide users with a way to get shortened URLs that they can paste into e-mail, Twitter, Facebook, or blogs. Embed URLs shortening services such as *bit.ly*.
- **Orphan Pages**: Search engines may index orphan pages or other sites may have links to orphan pages. Be sure to provide links on all orphan pages back to the web application's main (or home) page.
- **Non-Standard Link Colors**: Follow generally accepted color and display standard for links, *e.g.*, light blue with underlined text.
- **Outdated Information**: Update pages frequently. Outdated information reduces trust in the web application.
- **Lack of Navigation Support**: Allow users to navigate to various parts of the site. Be sure to provide a link to the "home" page from every page. A common standard is to include a logo on each page that is linked to the home page. Each page should also contain a "breadcrumb trail" that shows all the pages in the list of links that led to this page. An example of a "breadcrumb trail" is show in Figure 17.

The Cathris Group > Home > Education > Business & Systems Analysis > BA309

FIGURE 17. BREADCRUMB TRAIL FOR WEB SITE NAVIGATION

Other usability issues to consider include:

- **Contact Information**: Is it easy to find contact information, such as mailing address, customer service phone and e-mail, customer support phone and e-mail, and reporting site defects. Figure 18 shows an example.
- **Common Tasks**. Are common tasks easy to find? What are the common tasks that users need?

Phone: (978) 394-0597 | E-Mail: info@cathris.com
Site Map | Web Site Feedback | ©The Cathris Group, 2008. All Right Reserved.

FIGURE 18. CONTACT INFORMATION FOR WEB SITE

Testing Security

Web applications that collect information must be careful about protecting sensitive user information. Note that any form data that is submitted is sent to the web server over the Internet in plain text. Sensitive data must be encrypted. Form submission URLs must use the protocol prefix "https://" to ensure that information is encrypted.

Common Vulnerabilities

SQL Injection

SQL Injection is a common form of unsanitized user input where a web server is fooled into running an unintended SQL command that could retrieve unauthorized information from the database.

These types of attacks exploits faults in the implementation of embedded SQL commands in server-side scripts. For example, let's say that a programmer developed a feature that allowed users to retrieve a lost password by e-mailing it to them. The server-side code might look somewhat like this depending on the actual programming language in use:

```
QuQ
```

The expectation is that the uid variable contains the input value supplied by a user through a form field. The user is expected to enter an e-mail address or a user name. Now what would the SQL statement look like if the user types in this string instead:

Foo' OR 'x'='x

This is a tautology and is always true, so all rows in the Accounts table will be returned. Depending on how the script handles a multi-record result set, we might get all passwords or perhaps the first one.

Of course, now that we know that the website is vulnerable to SQL injection, we can use embedded SQL commands to do all sorts of database manipulation, *e.g.*, insert new rows, drop tables, alter tables, and so forth.

This vulnerability exists for ASP, JSP, PHP, and other server-side programming languages. What can be done about it? Sanitize the input and look for embedded SQL commands. Check that the input conforms to your expectations. Use different SQL execution schemes such as PREPARED statements. Segregate the database into multiple databases and protect tables with different security privileges. Finally, use stored procedures for database access rather than embedded SQL commands.

Steve Friedl's Unixwiz blog shows examples of SQL Injection attacks (Friedl, 2007). His website also contain links to other resources on SQL injection.

Web Testing Tools

The table below lists a number of useful web page testing tools. All of the tools are online apps that do not require installation of any client code.

TABLE 8. LIST OF USEFUL WEB TESTING TOOLS

Tool	Description
www.notableapp.com	Tool to capture web pages directly from a browser

	and then have ability to mockup the captured image and share with others.
tools.pingdom.com	Load testing of web pages with full reporting of each page component's load time.
www.webpagetest.org	Another page load testing tool with capability to test from different parts of the world. Also contains ability to test load time from mobile devices.
validator.w3.org	Check the markup validity of web document in HTML, XHTML, SMIL, MathML, CSS. Finds broken links and other coding issues.
browsershots.org	Provides screen shots of the output of a web page on virtually every browser for every platform.

Summary

- Links, images, color, fonts, and forms must be tested
- Usability and performance are important quality of service requirements for web applications and must be thoroughly evaluated
- Web applications must be tested on all target browsers and platforms

Quality Assurance Practices

Upon completion of this chapter you will be able to:

✓ List the different types of reviews
✓ Apply peer reviews to improve the "built-in" quality of solutions

Motivation

Most testers focus on dynamic testing where they run tests and observe the behavior the solution. Static testing, a quality assurance practice, is an analysis of the solution's implementation and the processes that lead to the development of the solution. The analysis is carried out through reviews and manual inspection of development artifacts. Static analysis of the code is also done manually, although some organizations employ static analysis tools for that purpose.

The main objective of static testing is to ensure that quality is "built in" and that the entire solution development process leads to a solution that meets the needs of the user and conforms to the stated requirements.

The goal of quality assurance practices is to find defects and deviations from not only the requirements specification, but also from project plans, organizational standards, regulations, and contractual agreements. Essentially, quality assurance is a collection of defect prevention practices – locate defects before they have a chance to affect the behavior the solution and before such abnormal behavior must be found through testing. Remember that one cannot test the entire solution – dynamic testing, by its very nature, is a sampling effort and there are always defects that will slip through those sampling cracks.

Reviews

Reviews rely on the analytical skills of people. Reviewers are expected to read artifacts and through analysis find potential defects or deviations from the specification.

Artifacts to Reviews

In general, all artifacts should be reviewed in at least some way, including models, requirements, prototypes, mockups, test cases, code modules, interface screens, web pages, use cases, and so forth.

Types of Reviews

In practice, there are several types of reviews differing in the level of formality and depth. Peer and stakeholder reviews are most common. Table 9 lists the different types of reviews.

TABLE 9. TYPES OF REVIEWS

Type of Review	Description
Peer Review	Peer reviews are conducted between the author of a document, design artifact, model, code module, or other solution artifact and his or her colleagues.
Stakeholder Walkthroughs	Reviews of requirements, models, mockups, or prototypes by stakeholder to verify that the requirements are correct.
Inspection	A formal review that generally evaluates a random subset of artifacts.
Audit	A formal inspection conducted by an outside review party to assure regulatory or organizational compliance.

Peer Reviews

The solution artifact's author and his or her colleagues conduct peer reviews. The goals are to assess the level of quality of the artifact and to point out areas where the artifact may have flaws that could lead to defects and where the artifact may not fully implement the requirements specification. Adherence to coding or other preparation standards and templates is another objective of peer reviews.

Peer reviews should be conducted frequently and as soon as an artifact has been developed. There is a simple mantra for peer reviews: find defects early before they have a chance to get into the solution and before dynamic testing has to sniff them out.

There are many other benefits to peer reviews:

- Finding and eliminating defects is often faster and generally much less expensive compared to dynamic testing leading to increased productivity.
- Development time is shortened, as less time has to be spent finding defects through exhaustive testing. Regression tests will turn up fewer defects that then need to be repaired.
- The quality of the solution will increase and fewer latent defects will exist.
- Reviews lead to mutual learning and knowledge transfer. The solution implementation team can improve their software process.
- Having multiple people look at solution artifacts and comparing them to the requirements specification results in alternate interpretations of the

specification. Ambiguities and misunderstanding are driven out much earlier in the development process.

- Quality becomes a group responsibility rather than the sole task of the artifact's author.

When conducting a peer review, it is important the remind everyone that it is the artifact that is being review and not the author. A moderator must facilitate the review. It is also advisable that managers not be included, so that frank discussions can be held without fear of repercussions.

Stakeholder Walkthrough

In a stakeholder walkthrough, the solution implementation team presents the requirements, test cases, models, and any mockups or prototypes to the stakeholders for review and verification. At the conclusion of the review, the stakeholders are expected to "sign-off" on the requirements to indicate their approval. The main outcome of a stakeholder review is assurance that the requirements have been understood correctly and that there is agreement is what capabilities of the delivered solution.

Inspection

An inspection is a more formal process conducted by an independent group of reviewers. Often sampling is employed and a random subset of artifacts is reviewed.

Audit

An audit is a formal inspection conducted by an outside group. Audits are often used in military or highly regulated industries such as medical device or pharmaceutical manufacturing.

Review Process

While there are different types of reviews, they are all conducted in a similar fashion and follow by and large the same overall process of plan, prepare, conduct, rework, and follow-up.

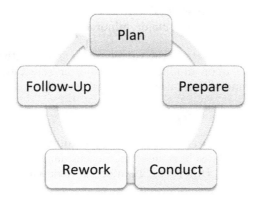

FIGURE 19. REVIEW PROCESS FOR QUALITY ASSURANCE

Plan Review

Decide which documents, models, code modules, prototypes, mockups, use cases, requirements, or other artifacts need to be reviewed. Estimate the effort and assure that there is sufficient time allocated in the project plan. The author of the artifact to be reviewed should select competent peers who can provide constructive feedback. The artifact to be reviewed must be in a reviewable state and sent to all review participants ahead to time.

Prepare

Prepare the logistics for the review meeting, including time, place, and necessary materials (whiteboards, projectors, print-outs, markers, highlighters, note cards, recording equipment.)

In addition, define the entry criteria for the meeting, i.e., what should have been done prior to the meeting, including any preparation expected by the participants. If the entry criteria are not met, cancel or reschedule the meeting as it is likely not going to be productive and would be a waste of precious project time.

Conduct

Conduct the review and encourage participants to share their opinions. Encourage participation and be sure to review the artifact and not personally attack the author. A skilled facilitator or moderator must manage the meeting; and that person should not be the author if at all possible. Issues uncovered during the review should be collected, recorded, but not resolved.

The review meeting should be limited to about 120 minutes. Larger artifacts may require multiple meetings. Consecutive meetings should have sufficient time between them to address issues. If a review is found to be ineffective due to lack of preparation or participation, it is critical that it be cancelled or postponed – do not waste anyone's time!

Issues raised during the review should be recorded, but not resolved and should be suggestions rather than specific directives. The author should have the opportunity to think about resolutions and seek advice outside the review meeting. Discovered defects should be categorized as critical, major, minor, or stylistic.

Upon conclusion of the meeting, the review team should either accept the artifact as is, accept it conditional upon modifications made, or reject the artifact as its quality is simply to sufficient and will require substantial rework.

Rework

The author should take any comments, issues pointed out, or defects uncovered and address them. Once updates have been made, another review should be conducted if the changes were significant. Otherwise, an informal review via e-mail or a smaller subset of reviewers is sufficient.

Follow-Up

The team should follow up to make sure the defects or issues have been addressed. The project manager should also make a note of the types of defects or issues that were discovered so that they can be added to checklists, templates, and other guidelines. If the same defects or issues are observed repeatedly, the project manager may schedule training or recommend the use of tools to minimize recurrence of the same issues or defects.

Summary

- Reviews are a form of static testing that ensure that quality is built-in from the outset
- Peer reviews and stakeholder walkthroughs are the most common form of review

Test Planning & Management

Upon completion of this chapter you will be able to:

✓ Create a test plan
✓ Define a defect severity classification scheme
✓ Select defect tracking and automated testing tools
✓ Collect measurements and produce quality metrics

Motivation

Testing is a critical aspect of solution development. The quality of a solution is directly related to the value the solution provides. Testing, therefore, must be methodical, efficient, and comprehensive yet mindful of the limited resources available for testing.

Testing Lifecycle

Figure 20 summarizes the testing process and overall lifecycle of the testing effort. A test plan defines how each stage of the lifecycle will be managed.

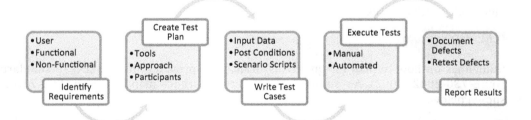

FIGURE 20. TESTING LIFECYCLE

Quality Control and Quality Assurance Planning

Planning should address quality control as well as quality assurance. An effective test team creates plans defining what work it expects to accomplish and what deliverables and time commitments it can make.

Standards

IEEE offers two standards (829 and 730) that offer guidelines for writing test and quality assurance plans. Note that they are guidelines and that they should be used as such. It is not advisable to follow them precisely unless required by the organization.

IEEE 829 Standard for Test Plans

Guidelines on how to write a test plan are provided in IEEE Standard 829 (IEEE 829-2008, 2008). A sample outline of a test plan based on IEEE 829 is provided below.

Test Plan

1. Test Version and Revision Identifier
2. Introduction
3. Test Items
4. Features to be tested
5. Features not to be tested
6. Testing Approach
7. Test Pass/Fail Criteria
8. Test Deliverables
9. Testing Tasks
10. Environmental Needs
11. Responsibilities
12. Staffing and Training Needs
13. Schedule
14. Risk and Contingencies
15. Approvals

Figure 21. Outline of Test Plan

IEEE 730 Standard for Quality Assurance

Guidelines on how to plan for quality assurance are provided in the IEE 730 standard (IEEE 730-2002, 2002). An outline for a quality assurance plan based on IEEE 730 is shown below.

Quality Assurance Plan

1. Purpose of the Plan
2. Reference Documents
3. Management of the Testing Effort
4. Standards, Practices, Conventions
5. Quality Metrics Collected
6. Static Reviews
7. Dynamic Testing Strategies
8. Defect Reporting Procedures
9. Testing, Tracking, and Reporting Tools
10. Media Control
11. Supplier Control
12. Records Collection, Maintenance, and Retention
13. Training
14. Risk Management
15. Glossary
16. SQAP Change Procedure and History

Wikis

The aforementioned plans do not have to be a printed document produced in a word processor. In fact, an actual document is difficult to manage, track, and update. A better way to publish plans is to use a wiki – a collaborative web site. A wiki is easily updatable by members of a group and comments can be left by anyone in the group. Instead of hunting down the latest version of a document, the wiki always contains the latest information. Naturally, wikis provide a history of changes so that version control becomes much simpler. Table lists some free cloud-based wikis, but internally hosted solutions are available as well.

TABLE 10. LIST OF WIKIS FOR PLAN PUBLICATION

Wiki	Features & Highlights
www.wikia.com	A simple to use and free wiki platform with quick templates to get started.
www.wikidot.com	A more comprehensive commercial wiki platform. Offers a free plan as well.
wiki.zoho.com	A wiki that is part of the Zoho suite; links to spreadsheets, documents, files, bugs, etc. One wiki is free, more cost money.

| www.wikispaces.com | A pay for use hosted wiki solution with lots of industrial grade features such as revision tracking and private labeling. |

Test Prioritization

Because time and resources for testing are limited, not all tests can be executed sufficiently and fully. Therefore, it is necessary to select test cases that should be focused on. Prioritization ensures that should testing have to end prematurely (perhaps due to time or money running out), the most important tests have been performed. Table 11 lists some of the most common criteria for prioritizing tests.

TABLE 11. TEST PRIORITIZATION CRITERIA

Criterion	Justification
Usage Frequency	Features that are more commonly used have a higher impact should they fail, so they should be tested earlier.
Risk Score	Each test should assess the likelihood that a component might fail and the impact that failure would have. The product of these two values is the risk score. Components with high-risk scores should be tested early.
Visibility	Failures that are visible to the end users should be addressed early.
Business Impact	Failures that have a negative impact on business, such as lost sales or compromised reputation, should be address early.
Complexity	Components that contain complex rules or complex technical implementations are more likely to have an increased number of defects and therefore should be addressed early.
Requirements Priority	Test cases that test high priority requirements should themselves have higher priority to assure that a such a feature is delivered at a high level of quality.

Defect Severity Classification

An important criterion when judging the significance of a reported defect is the impact it is anticipated to have on the viability of the solution. IEEE Standard 1044 (IEEE 1044-1993, 1993) defines a severity classification scheme and a variant of that scheme is shown in Table 12.

TABLE 12. DEFECT SEVERITY CLASSIFICATION SCHEME

Class	Potential Impact	Releasable?
1 – FATAL	The solution does not continue to function and possible loss of data or life is possible	No
2 –SEVERE	A key requirement has not been fulfilled and the functionality is significantly impaired for important stakeholders; requires expensive or onerous workarounds to be usable	No
3 – SERIOUS	A requirement is only partially available or somewhat incorrect; significant impact to some stakeholders; solution is usable but has severe restrictions	No
4 – MODERATE	Some minimal flaws in the implementation of less important requirements; system is usable but has minor annoyances	Yes (but with caveats)
5 – MINOR	Insignificant impact on a few stakeholders with minimal impact to functionality	Yes (but with caveats)

Defect Tracking

As discussed in previously, defects must be recorded as they are discovered. The IEEE Standard for Software Test Documentation ((IEEE 829-2008, 2008) defines a document called an incident report whose purpose is "document any event that occurs during the testing process which requires investigation." The standard does not prescribe any particular template for a defect report. Table 6 summarizes the main elements of a defect incident report.

Defects discovered during testing must be recorded and details of the test and the unexpected result must be communicated to the solution development team. The report must include sufficient information for the solution team to understand the defect and be able to replicate it. It is expected that supporting documentation such as screen shots or narrated screen casts are included in the report. Tools such as *SnagIt*, *Snipping Tool*, or other screen capturing tools are often used to produce screen shots. Screen casting tools capture entire interactions as a replayable video. Tools such as screenr.com, *JingIt*, *ComStudio*, *Camtasia*, *iMovie*, or *Hypercam* are useful for this purpose.

Defect Tracking Tools

While manual forms might work on small projects, larger efforts require automated defect and general incident tracking. Searching, sorting, reporting, tracking, and storing are cumbersome with paper forms. Luckily, there are numerous "bug tracking" databases available on the market, many of which are free or very low cost. Some are

89

cloud-based tools while others require local installation with shared databases on servers. A selection of free as well as commercial tools is listed in Table 13; many more can be found with simple web searches[6].

TABLE 13. AUTOMATED DEFECT TRACKING TOOLS

Tool	Cost	Cloud?	Description
Bugzilla	Free	No	A web-based bug tracking system with many features; a widely used tool, particularly on open-source projects; highly configurable
SourceForge.net	Free	Yes	Widely used open source and online bug tracking system with many features
FogBugz	$25/lic/mo	Yes	A simple to use, powerful, and robust tool
Zoho BugTracker	$40/lic/mo	Yes	A powerful defect tracking tool that integrates with Zoho's suite of project management and productivity tools
Mantis	Free	No	A web-based system that is lightweight, simple, and configurable

In the above table, $$$ means more than $500 per license, $$ means between $100 and $499 per license, and $ means less than $100 per license. Note that cloud-based tools are often licensed per user per month.

Traceability

Requirements should be traceable to specific test cases that can determine if the requirement has been implemented properly. Likewise, each test case should be linked back the specific requirements that are being evaluated by this test case. The linkage between requirements and test cases is either managed manually through a spreadsheet or is automatically tracked by a test case management tool or automated testing system.

The traceability matrix also acts as a coverage matrix that project managers can use to determine which requirements have not yet been allocated to implementation. A more comprehensive requirements matrix also includes linkage to business objectives to ensure that all included requirements actually address a business need.

---

[6] For example, http://aptest.com/bugtrack.html contains a comprehensive list of cloud-based as well as desktop based defect tracking tools.

				Requirements & Use Cases		
		R001	R002	UC01	UC02	...	UC43

	R001	R002	UC01	UC02	...	UC43
T001		x	x			
T002		x		x		
...						
T296	x					

Test Cases (row axis label)

In lieu of a full traceability matrix, each test case can simply reference the requirements it tests and each requirement description can simply contain the test cases that evaluate it. If the test cases and requirements are stored in a requirements management system then the traceability matrix can be constructed by the tool as a report.

Automated Testing

The same tests often have to be run over and over whenever a new feature is introduced as that enhancement may introduce new defects and lead to unwanted side effects. The process of re-running tests periodically is called *regression testing*.

Even small projects may have hundreds of tests cases – just think of all of the equivalence classes that can be built from a simple use case. Re-running the same tests repeatedly is not only time consuming, but takes testers away from creating and running tests for the new features or performing quality of service testing.

Software testing tools and test automation robots can help address this problem by providing a more efficient and less labor intensive way to perform regression testing.

Macro Recorders

In an automated test environment, a computer program takes the role of a tester and generates keystrokes and mouse clicks the same way a human would. The program being tested does not know the difference; the test tool is completely *non-invasive*.

In the simplest case, a test engineer uses a macro recorder to run a test normally but have the recorder save all keystrokes and mouse actions. Then the macro can be played back as needed. Of course, if the interface changes, then the macro has to be re-recorded. Table 14 lists a few of more commonly used macro recorders for Windows and Mac.

TABLE 14. MACRO RECORDER TOOLS TO TEST AUTOMATION

Tool	Platform	Price	Highlights & Features
QuicKeys	Mac OS X 10.5 or earlier	$60	Records keystrokes and mouse actions as shortcuts that can be saved and played back. Presently not compatible with Mac OS X 10.7 (Lion)
Macro Magic	Windows	$150	Records keystrokes and mouse actions as sharable macros

By the way, even a small change in the position of a window or text box can throw off the recorder. Make sure that an application and its pop-up dialogs appear always in exactly the same spot – mouse clicks are recorded as absolute positions. Be sure to update any macros after interface changes.

These recorders are not just useful for automated testing, but can alleviate any other monotonous task.

Programmable Testing Tools

In order to react to different screen positions or changes in the test path, a more flexible macro must be created. An automated testing tool generally contains a macro programming language that can encode the full test script and all of its scenarios. The tester specifies the correct outputs and the testing tools looks for those outputs.

Tool	Highlights & Features
HP QuickTest	A scalable and unified quality assurance and automated testing platform; provides metrics and graphs, manages defects, and executes tests automatically
SilkTest	Provides for automated execution of role-based test scripts; includes browser testing for web applications
Rational Robot	Comprehensive testing tools for functional testing at the source level; integrates with other Rational products such as *Rational ClearQuest* for defect management
Selenium	An open source (and free) platform for automated testing of browser-based applications
QA Wizard	Automated functional and load testing of web applications
SOATest	Testing of SOA layers including functionality, performance, security and policy enforcement
OpenLoad	An open source load testing platform available through

	SourceForge
Testing Master	A tool for web site stress, load, and speed testing

These tools require the construction of complex test scripts in a scripting language. Therefore, programming experience is necessary to operate these automated testing tools.

In addition to the automators listed in this section, there are other tools or services that can be used for distributed load, stress, and volume testing. The *Microsoft Stress Utility* is an example.

Configuration Management

A software solution is a collection of interconnected components that must all be tested together to ensure that the solution works as planned. Changes made to the configuration of the test environment must be carefully documented.

The solution must also be tested on different operating systems and hardware configurations. Virtualization can help in cutting down on the number of physical machines needed to test different operating environment.

Quality Metrics

Storing discovered defects in a database opens many possibilities for reporting and measuring the health of not only the testing effort, but also overall project health. By using a defect tracking system, queries can be issued against the database to analyze the collected defect data. Such measurements are generally referred to as *metrics*.

Among the most common queries performed by testers are searching for specific defects, defects in certain versions of the software or defect of a certain criticality. Other queries might zoom in on defects that were repaired or are still open, defects that were assigned to a particular person to fix, or defects reported by a particular tester.

The queries results can also be turned into measurements, such as the average number of defects discovered per tester or the number of defects discovered per day. The results of these metrics can then be turned into reports, charts, graphs, or displayed on dashboards. For example, Figure 23 shows the distribution of defects by severity.

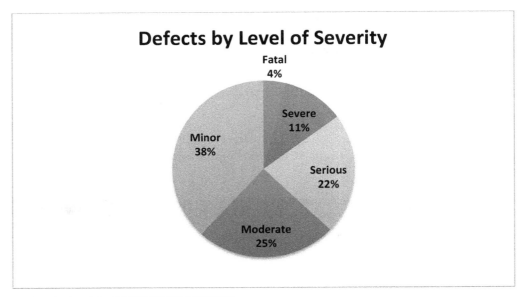

FIGURE 23. CHART OF DEFECTS BY SEVERITY

Common Project-Level Metrics

Gauging the health and progress of a project is an important management activity. Metrics can provide insight into progress and allow managers to see if the project might miss its schedule, run over budget, or fail to deliver its promised level of quality. Table 15 lists some of the more common project metrics.

TABLE 15. COMMON PROJECT METRICS

Metric	Definition	Use/Interpretation
Defect Discovery Rate	Number of defects discovered per time period, *e.g.*, defects per day or defects per week. Can be done by defect severity, *i.e.*, serious	The defect discovery rate initially rises, but should eventually plateau and then drop. Release should not be before it reaches its plateau.
Aggregate Total Defects	Number of unresolved defects remaining; can be segmented by defect severity	Shows the net difference between the defect discovery rate and the defect repair rate
Defect Resolution Rate	Number of defects resolved per time period	Articulates the productivity of the development team
Defect Density	Number of defects open and/or closed for some part of the solution or some module	Illustrates the distribution of defects across different parts of the solution; may point out relative strength of different

	development teams; may also indicate uneven test effort

The charts and graphs below illustrate some of the above metrics with examples. Note that these metrics and charts are most likely built by the test manager or project manager rather than testers, test designers, or business analysts.

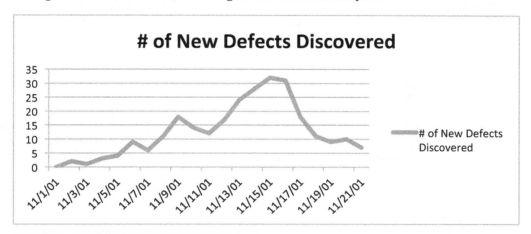

FIGURE 24. NEW DEFECTS DISCOVERED EACH DAY

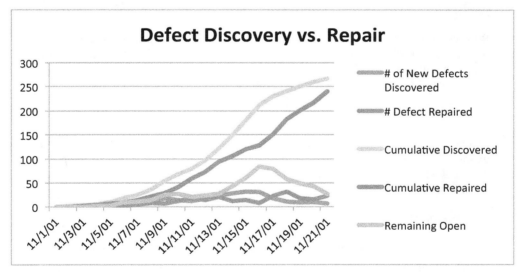

FIGURE 25. DEFECT DISCOVERY VERSUS REPAIR

Testing When Resources are Limited

Testing is a labor intensive and time consuming effort and even the best tools can take the sting out of it. Automated testing tools can only run a test defined by a test engineer and the tests are only as good as the test designer. People have intuition and can exercise the software in unexpected ways. The more testers interact with the software, the more likely it is that the most critical defects are discovered.

Bug Bashes

A bug bash is a fun way for the entire team to participate in testing. The team might take a few hours and everyone on the team runs tests or does exploratory testing. In an effective bug bash, some small part of the solution is selected for intensive testing; the idea is to focus resources and really dig into some module or set of functionality.

To make the bug bash even more effective, introduce games. Divide the team into smaller groups, have each group select a group name, and then offer prizes to the group that discovers the most bugs or has the most number of defects of some kind.

Bug bashes often reveal lots about the usability of the solution. If the interface was poorly designed, the bug bashers will run into problems carrying out their tests. It might be worthwhile to observe the bashers to see where they run into usability barriers.

Beta Testing

A bug bash is a sort of internal beta test, where the solution is used by lots of people other than the developers. Beta testing extends this to external parties and potential users. Beta testing occurs generally at the end of the development lifecycle when the product is considered to be substantially complete.

Be sure to monitor that beta users are actually using the product. Otherwise, there might be few if any bug reports and the development team might draw the incorrect conclusion that the solution is defect-free when in fact it has simply not been used enough. Once again, incentives can increase beta testing participation.

Crowd Testing

Crowd testing is a newer form of testing that leverages social networks and the web. For example, Pay4Bugs.com is a global marketplace where developers can offer a bounty for each defect discovered. Testers from all over the world sign up and then earn money by testing products that have been submitted for testing.

Outsourced Testing

A common practice when testing resources or expertise are in short supply is to outsource testing to an external firm, perhaps even to an offshore specialty firm. Outsourced testing requires good and very complete specifications. As those are often not available, outsourced testing may focus on other types of testing, such as usability, configuration, compatibility, and localization testing.

Communication with the outsourcing partner is very important, so be sure to establish proper expectations, expected reports, and a shared defect repository.

Summary

- Test planning assures that the testing effort is carried out methodically and in a repeatable manner
- A traceability matrix links requirements to test cases and vice versa
- Automated testing can reduce the labor involved in managing and executing test cases
- Defect tracking systems are databases that store test incidents; these databases can be queried and searched
- Collecting quality metrics can help in assessing project health and the productivity and efficacy of the testing effort
- Use outsourcing, crowdsourcing, bug bashes, and beta tests to leverage others

Final Thoughts

Upon completion of this chapter you will be able to:

✓   Understand how all of the different techniques relate

✓   Determine if the techniques covered help address your testing challenges

Review & Conclusions

In this course we had a chance to learn about:

- The difference between quality control and quality assurance
- The different types of testing strategies
- The value of test planning and management
- The value of boundary analysis, equivalence partitioning, decision tables, and state charting to guide test scenario development
- Quality assurance techniques, including static reviews

Principals of Successful Testing

Let's summarize the major principles of successful testing that we explored in this course:

1. **The objective of testing is to identify defects and not prove that the solution works**. The successful testers works under the assumption that the requirements are incomplete, inaccurate, and misunderstood and that the solution is therefore flawed.
2. **The goal of testing is to locate as many defects as possible in the allotted time**. Due to time, budget, and other resource constraints, it is not feasible to discover all defects. The solution team and the project sponsor must agree on an acceptable level of quality.
3. **Fully define the expected outcome of each test case by creating a test case definition**. Define test suites aid in regression testing and when automating the test process.
4. **Testers and test designers should be as removed from the solution implementation team as possible**. An external party is more likely to define unusual and unorthodox test cases that exercise the boundary conditions and likely make fewer implicit assumptions. Above all, developers and programmers should not perform their own acceptance testing.
5. **Use case scenarios combined with equivalence class partitioning define the most effective test cases**. Identify the basic path, alternate paths, and exception paths as well as combinations of paths from the use cases. Identify boundary conditions and create additional test cases.

6. **Track test plans, test cases, and test results**. All test artifacts should be written and tracked in a repository, ideally a test database. Defects should be tracked in a defect management system.

7. **Focus testing on where defects are most likely**. Most defects occur at the edges of boundary conditions and where issues have arisen in the past. Focus testing efforts on those areas if time is limited.

8. **Be mindful of side effects**. When updates or changes are made to a solution, check that all previous functionality still works as expected. Perform regression testing by re-running all tests if necessary.

9. **Verify the requirements before testing**. Test cases and test plans should be based on defined and verified requirements. Review all requirements with stakeholders and obtain their approval.

10. **Create a safe test environment**. Do not run tests in the production environment, but rather execute them in a safe test environment that mimics the actual production environment as closely as possible.

11. **Assure quality throughout**. Testing catching many but not all mistakes in the implementation of the solution. Quality can be significantly improved by conducting static testing in the form of requirements, design, and code reviews prior to implementation.

Course Evaluation

Complete the online course evaluation at http://www.cathris.com/eval or scan the QR Code for quicker access. Use the course code provided by your instructor.

Appendix A: Job Aids

Electronic versions of the job aids are available by request through jobaids@cathris.com. You may freely use these templates, process guide, and checklists. If you come up with a particularly good new job aid, consider sharing it with your community.

Job Aid 1. Writing Effective Requirements using *SMART*

Applicability

This job aid is used during requirements reviews and is part of quality assurance. It specifies how to write effective requirements

Checklist

Requirement ID:

Attribute	Definition	Assessment	Actions
Specific	The requirement is specific, atomic, and does not contain vague terms.		
Measurable	The requirement can be measured.		
Achievable	The requirement can be attained and is feasible.		
Relevant	The requirement can be traced back to a need or objective.		
Testable	The requirement has one or more test cases associated with it.		

Usage

During the requirements review, apply this checklist to every requirement. Check if each attribute is met and record the assessment. If it is not met, record any actions that need to be taken.

Job Aid 2. Component Testing Checklist

Applicability

This job aid is used during code reviews and to prepare dynamic component tests.

Checklist

	Criterion	Definition
☐	*Correctness*	The code is deemed to be correct; it produces the correct result for expected inputs
☐	*Robustness*	The code fails gracefully when incorrect input is presented
☐	*Exception Handling*	The code has a handler for every possible exception
☐	*Reachability*	All statements in the component can be reached
☐	*Memory Management*	Memory for temporary object is released properly after the last use of the object
☐	*Efficiency*	The code is efficiently designed and is expected to work as input volume increases; the data structures used are appropriate for the amount of data expected to be processed; the run-time behavior of the data structure is known
☐	*Maintainability*	The code can be maintained by a third party; routine maintenance and updates can be performed by someone other than the programmer
☐	*Documentation*	The code is well documented; each statement block is explained and the code follows commenting standards
☐	*Code Standards*	The code follows organizational code standards
☐	*Test Harness*	A test harness has been written for this code
☐	*Source Controlled*	The code has been checked into the source control system and is under configuration management
☐	*No Hardcoding*	Parameters, counters, and other configurable values are in settable variables

Job Aid 3. Defect Report

Applicability

This job aid is used to record information about defects discovered during testing. Defect tracking tools may have their own format and set of attributes for a defect report.

Template

Defect Report

Submitted On:	_____	*Submitted By:*	_____
Discovered On:	_____	*Discovered By:*	_____
Version:	_____	*Status:*	_____
Application/Page:	_____	*Priority:*	_____
Defect Type:	_____	*Date Resolved:*	_____
Module/Page:	_____	*Severity:*	_____

Detailed Description

Script/Trace

Action	*Response*	*Screen Shot*

Attachments

Sample

Defect Report

Submitted On:	11/23/2011	*Submitted By:*	Glen Marcus
Discovered On:	11/21/2011	*Discovered By:*	Client Bug Report
Version:	June 2010	*Status:*	Open
Application:	BoatVentures	*Priority:*	Low
Module/Page:	view-yachts.html	*Severity:*	Not Critical
Defect Type:	Usability/Content	*Date Resolved:*	

Detailed Description

The pictures for yachts are too big and are not scaled to the available screen real estate.

Script/Trace

Action	*Response*	*Screen Shot*
Navigated to Work/View Yachts	List of yachts as expected, but images are too large	

Attachments

Job Aid 4. Web Usability Checklist

Applicability

This job aid is used during web application reviews.

Checklist

	Review Item
☐	All links resolve to their expected targets
☐	Images are of the correct size
☐	Page displays on all target browsers and screen size and orientations
☐	Links are distinguishable from standard text
☐	Images have an "alternate text"
☐	All images display
☐	No scrolling text or looping animations
☐	Navigation to "Home" is possible from all pages
☐	Breadcrumb trail is visible on each page
☐	Orphan pages have been resolved
☐	Forms submit properly
☐	Forms reset properly
☐	Error messages on incorrectly filled forms are instructional
☐	Plug-ins are available on all platforms
☐	Cookies do not contain private information

Job Aid 5. Use Case Template

Applicability

This job aid is used to record a use case narrative with its normal, alternate, and exception scenarios.

Template

Title:	<use case name/title>	*Identifier:*	<unique id>

Description:	<short description of the use case; often expressed as an agile user story>

Author:		*Version:*	*Priority:*
Perspective:	<current or future state>		*Type:*
Duration:		*Frequency:*	*Status:*

Pre Conditions:	• <list of pre conditions>
Scenarios:	• <list of scenarios>
Example Scenario:	<narrative of an example>
Normal Path:	<list of steps in the normal path or the basic/normal scenario>
Variations:	<list of variations>
Post Conditions:	<list of post conditions>

Related Requirements & Rules	<list of related or applicable requirements and/or business rules>

Open Issues & Notes:	<any applicable notes, constraints, assumptions, or other information that can aid the implementer>

Bibliography

Black, R. (2007). *Pragmatic Software Testing.* Indianapolis: Wiley Publishing, Inc.

Friedl, S. (2007, October 10). *SQL injection attacks by example.* Retrieved November 27, 2011, from UnixWiz.Net Tech Tips: http://www.unixwiz.net/techtips/sql-injection.html

Gheorghiu, G. (2005, February 28). *Performance vs. load vs. stress testing.* Retrieved November 26, 2011, from Agile Testing: http://agiletesting.blogspot.com/2005/02/performance-vs-load-vs-stress-testing.html

IEEE 1008-1987. (1987). *Standard for Software Unit Testing.* Washington: IEEE.

IEEE 1012-1998. (1998). *Standard for Software Verification and Validation.* Washington: IEEE.

IEEE 1028-2008. (2008). *Standard for Software Reviews and Audits.* Washington: IEEE.

IEEE 1044-1993. (1993). *Standard Classification for Software Anomalies.* Washington: IEEE.

IEEE 1219-1998. (1998). *Standard for Software Maintenance.* Washington: IEEE.

IEEE 12207-2008. (2008). *Information Technology - Software Lifecycle Processes.* Washington: IEEE.

IEEE 730-2002. (2002). *Standard for Software Quality Assurance.* Washington: IEEE.

IEEE 828-2005. (2002). *Standard for Software Configuration Management Plans.* Washington: IEEE.

IEEE 829-2008. (2008). *Standard for Software and System Test Documentation.* Washington: IEEE.

IEEE 830-1998. (1998). *Recommended Practices for Software Requirements Specification.* Washington: IEEE.

McCaffrey, J. (2009). *Software Testing: Fundamental Principles and Essential Knowledge.* Book Surge.

Meier, J., Farre, C., Bansode, P., Barber, S., & Rea, D. (2007). *Performance Testing Guidance for Web Applications.* Redmond, WA, USA: Microsoft Press.

Nielsen, J. (2000, March 19). *Why You Only Need to Test with 5 Users.* Retrieved November 27, 2011, from useIT: http://www.useit.com/alertbox/20000319.html

Patton, R. (2006). *Software Testing.* Indianapolis: Sams Publishing.

Software Certifications. (2006). *CSTE Common Body of Knowledge.* Quality Assurance Institute.

Spillner, A., Linz, T., & Schaefer, H. (2011). *Software Testing Foundations.* Santa Barbara, CA: Rocky Nook.

About The Cathris Group

The Cathris Group is a technology education and consulting practice with a focus on helping IT organizations maximize their effectiveness through the practical application of modern and proven approaches. Founded in 2001 by Dr. Martin Schedlbauer, *The Cathris Group* has built a strong reputation for excellence in training, business analysis and software implementation. Its cost-effective programs have been delivered worldwide for a diverse set of clients.

Core Competencies

We have over 20 years of experience in developing client-focused training and knowledge adoption solutions. Our training programs are drawn from our consulting engagements and are therefore presented in a practical manner with real-world examples. Our course materials are written in-house and can be tailored to each client. We can create custom materials for our clients to use in their own training programs.

We are skilled in all aspects of modern business analysis and information systems development, including modeling, agile methods, the Unified Modeling Language (UML), the Business Analysis Body of Knowledge (BABOK®), business process modeling (BPM) with BPMN and UML, use case analysis, requirements elicitation and management, quantitative operations, business case, and process analysis, and technical implementation in various languages and technologies.

Service Offerings

- Custom On-site Training & Education
- Business Process Modeling
- Agile Project Coaching
- Custom Courseware Authoring
- Executive Briefings
- Consulting
- Methodology Development
- Quantitative Analysis (Cost-Benefit, Process)
- Research

Areas of Expertise

Business Systems Analysis

Business Analysis Skills · Elicitation · Requirements Management · Use Cases · Data and Information Modeling · Business Rules · Business Process Modeling · UML · BPMN · Agile Business Analysis · Scrum · Discovery Prototyping Business Case Analysis · Quality Assurance & Testing

Information Systems Development

Object-Oriented Analysis & Design · UML · Agile/Scrum · Relational Database Design · SQL · Java · XML · C++ · HTML · Web Application Development · Mobile App Development · Objective C · xCode/Cocoa

www.cathris.com ■ info@cathris.com

www.ingramcontent.com/pod-product-compliance
Lightning Source LLC
Chambersburg PA
CBHW080430060326
40689CB00019B/4452